What Others Are Saying

This book is a great source of life for many people. It tells you that you are not alone in your struggles. If "Angel's" family can be free and healed, so can you! Turn to the Lord as they did! Let Him give you the strength! Trust in Him and He will bring you through. Remember, you can do all things and live because of Him. I pray you will receive all hope and blessings this book can bring you!

Delores Winder
Bill and Delores Winder Ministry
http://www.deloreswinder.com/

The Walking Wounded reveals the paralyzing cycle of domestic violence with raw and courageous candor. Every chapter is both compelling and educational, capturing a rare insight into the reaction (and/ or lack of action) by a victim. *Walking Wounded* is a testament to those who are currently struggling with their own domestic nightmare that they are not alone in their battle—to be encouraged and strengthened by the saving grace of Christ.

Shannon Deitz
Hopeful Hearts Ministry
www.hopefulheartsministry.com

The book is powerful and moving with a level of transparency that is quite freeing to the reader. I believe thousands of women and men alike will find their freedom by reading it.

Pastor D. Dunn, River Outreach Center

You are about to embark upon a journey involving domestic violence through the eyes of the abused spouse. In *The Walking Wounded*, Secret Angel paints a picture for us all to learn lessons and gain knowledge about the dynamics of domestic violence. The goal is to spare many from calamity and shed light on this type of human suffering.

The Walking Wounded is written in an easy to understand way that reveals the thoughts, feelings and pain the abused spouse encounters at each juncture in her life with the abuser.

Truth in our pain is the pathway to wholeness and a necessary step to fulfilling our destiny. Grace takes us to truth so that we can face pain, become whole and fulfill our call here on Earth. From brokenness to the quest for wholeness, we will follow Secret Angel's life and gleam many valuable lessons as light is shown on a path. A life now destined for greatness once thought to be too broken to be loved or used.

Rhonda Waldrop—A friend, a connection, that God has so graciously allowed to watch a beautiful transformation process.

Secret Angel has powerfully described the life of a victim of abuse. She has been led by the Holy Spirit in writing this book. She has bared her soul at a very deep and painful level. As a victim of abuse she knows the horror, trauma and the deep pain of rejection, abandonment and betrayal. She has articulately described a journey of deep despair as a victim of abuse to a Woman of God brought out of the pits of hell to a life of Hope and Restoration. This book is for everyone to read ... hope to the abused ... and understanding to the abuser of the damage and destruction of the life you say you love and care about.

Carolyn Puckett, LCSW
Freedom Counseling Center
Pineville, Louisiana

"If you want to know what HELL ON EARTH is like?—READ THIS TRUE STORY!! After you read it, you will see what the devil is like and how he uses all of us for his own evil endeavors. I sat next to this woman for almost 20 years. We worked together; we were friends; our children were our priorities! Little did I know the HELL that my friend was going through!!"

Mary Ellen Pauley

Secret Angel's book "THE WALKING WOUNDED" has helped me to heal. I read her poem on WordPress and it touched me right away. SO MUCH HURT! SO MUCH PAIN! "THE WALKING WOUNDED!" THAT'S THEIR NAME!

After reading her book, I can truly say that God is still in control, and He makes ways where there were no ways. I found myself diving in to read chapter after chapter. And then I would have to stop and receive the healing that God put in her words. Angel is so honest, so truthful about what it feels like to live in abuse. She shares with such passion and emotion what really goes on behind closed doors with an Abuser. There were many times I just stopped reading and cried—for me and for her.

Angel also shares how God directed her every move to stay safe and get out. Provision, protection, and deliverance—are all in her book. Her story is an amazing testimony of what God can do when we cry out to him for help. It touched my heart and gives me hope for the many, many women she will help set free. I would recommend this book to anyone and everyone who is or knows someone in an abusive relationship. There is healing here! Secret Angel and I collaborated and released the song "WALKING WOUNDED" based on her poem. It is available at CD Baby.

Diana Rasmussen
Prayers and Promises
Music Minister, Blogger, Poetess, and Recording Artist

THE WALKING WOUNDED

The Path From Brokenness To Wholeness

By "Secret Angel"

The Walking Wounded
Fully Surrendered
Copyright © 2013 Secret Angel, Inc.
ISBN: 978-0-9836-109-46
www.SecretAngelMinistry.org

Bush Publishing & Associates books may be ordered at www.BushPublishing.com or www.Amazon.com. For further information, please contact:
Bush Publishing & Associates
www.BushPublishing.com

Design by Kiefer Likens
Photography by JB Photography
Layout by The Ambush Group / www.TheAmbushGroup.com

This book is dedicated to all my family and friends who have stood by me and prayed for me as I walked this path from brokenness to wholeness.

It is also dedicated to my Heavenly Father, who rescued me when I did not even know that I needed rescuing.

Finally, I dedicate this book to all the abused people in this country and around the world. I pray for their salvation, deliverance, healing, and restoration, and I pray that each one will go from being a victim to being an overcomer.

"The Lord is close to the brokenhearted...
He rescues those who are crushed in spirit."
(Psalm 34:18)

*I wish to express my heartfelt thanks to all of the prayer warriors
who have prayed for me and with me over these years during
my lowest points of brokenness and through my journey to wholeness.
It is through these prayers that my children and I were saved and
reintroduced to our Mighty God who makes the impossible, possible.
I know that God is no respecter of persons, and what He has
done for me and my children, will do for others.*

Table of Contents

Introduction XVII

Chapter 1: The Walking Wounded 1

Chapter 2: The Years of Innocence 5

Chapter 3: The School Years 11

Chapter 4: Bullying 15

Chapter 5: Through the Looking Glass 19

Chapter 6: Newlyweds 25

Chapter 7: Marriage 35

Chapter 8: Wounds 47

Chapter 9: The Whirlwind Begins 55

Chapter 10: The Breakup 63

Chapter 11: The Impossible Task 69

Chapter 12: The Rollercoaster 75

Chapter 13: The Turmoil 81

Chapter 14: Divorce 91

Chapter 15: The Death Threat 95

Chapter 16: Getting Help 107

Chapter 17: Legal Battles 115

Chapter 18: The Perfect Storm 123

Chapter 19:   Reopening Doors 129

Chapter 20:   The Other Woman 133

Chapter 21:   Spiritual Abuse 137

Chapter 22:   Healing Begins 143

Chapter 23:   Financial Abuse 149

Chapter 24:   Truth 155

Chapter 25:   More Truths 163

Chapter 26:   Fear 171

Chapter 27:   The Miraculous 177

Chapter 28:   Soul Ties 185

Chapter 29:   Moving Toward Healing 191

Chapter 30:   Obedience 197

Chapter 31:   Wholeness 201

               Editor's Note 205

               Prayer 209

INTRODUCTION

Praying for Guidance: The Confirmation

"Trust in the Lord with all your heart, do not depend on your own understanding. Seek his will in all you do, and He will direct your paths." Proverbs 3:5-6 (NLT)

Putting my life on paper is the hardest thing I have ever done. I stopped writing this book after the very first chapter because of the pain that it caused just to think of some of the things that I have been through. I didn't want to open that door to my past. I actually had written a book, filled with hurt, several years ago after living in fear when the one man that I ever loved threatened to kill me after a traumatic divorce. My whole life had been turned upside down. I kept it for years, never publishing it. I believed that no one would want to read about my life. Who would want to read about emotional and verbal abuse? I was just a normal person who was trying to live my life the best that I could in a world of hurt. I had written it for inner healing, not for people to read my deepest, darkest secrets. But now, after many years, I am being told again that I need to write a book about my life. Many questions filled my mind as I thought about this book. Then I questioned if this is what God wanted from my broken life. I didn't want to open those old doors of pain, hurt, and trauma back into my life for no purpose. I had painfully learned over the years that a major battle occurs in the mind—the battle of right versus wrong or good versus evil. I had survived the evil that came against me, and I did not want to dwell on my past struggles. I wanted to look forward to my future with hope and expectation. But, I realized that it's not about me. The question is what does God want? To answer the question, my oldest son and I prayed for direction and for God to clearly tell us what he wanted me to do before I continued past the first chapter. We got our answer the next day in the most interesting way.

As I was changing the channels on my mother's television for her, I clearly heard, *"I challenge you today to write your life story and do it now!"* I wondered where that statement came from. Well, I discovered that a Christian network had just been passed. I thought that I would still be on the safe side and prayed for more confirmation. I even called my son and sister to inform them what I heard and to be praying for more confirmation. I needed to make sure that God was telling me to write a book again. There were many tears shed as I had written the first chapter the night before, and I did not want to proceed unless it was definitely God's plan for my life.

Well, within an hour of getting home, I got a call from a friend. As we talked, she asked if I had heard about her husband's good news. I told her that I had not. She proceeded to inform me that her husband wrote a book and was having it published. When I asked her about it, she informed me that "God told him in January to write a book about his life. It's all about the abuse, pain, addictions, and everything he's survived throughout his life. God has healed him, and God wants to use him to help others!"

I told her that I had been praying for confirmation about the same thing. She told me that God wanted those of us who have been through these traumas and healed to reach out to others. She told me that God may want to use my story also to help others who have been abused.

These two confirmations occurred within hours of each other, and I became clear on the Lord's direction. He had spoken, and I would be obedient. Through the years, I learned the importance of walking in obedience when God says to do something. In fact, I have had to repent for not following through with the first book. At the time, I thought it was just for inner healing. Now, I realize that I am going through more abuse, a different type of abuse, so that my story can help others. I will continue to write this book, and I will dedicate it to all the abused people around this country and the world. I pray for their salvation, deliverance, healing, and restoration. I also pray that each one will go from being a victim to being an overcomer.

CHAPTER 1

The Walking Wounded

*"Jesus said, 'Father, forgive these people, because they
don't know what they are doing..."*
Luke 23:34(NLT)

There are so many people walking around in this world that go about their day to day activities appearing to be so normal and healthy. The only time someone might identify a problem is if a person has an obvious physical ailment. Unfortunately, there are many more people walking around with hidden wounds—wounds from physical abuse, emotional abuse, psychological abuse, verbal abuse, sexual abuse, financial abuse, and even spiritual abuse. I call these people, "The Walking Wounded."

"The Walking Wounded" actually have wounds that are deeper than physical wounds. These wounds are deep where the naked eye can't see them. They are not wounds that cause you to physically limp, but these wounds can actually make you emotionally stumble. Some of these wounds cut to the very soul and spirit of a person and can eventually cause physical ailments due to the effects of stress on the body. These wounded people go about their lives, hopefully functioning as normal as possible, until another abuse occurs or another trauma erupts in their lives. Then, they have to emotionally pull themselves together to go on with their lives again. Some become assertive and confront the situation. However, some become more passive, always trying to please everyone to avoid confrontation.

Many of these wounds can begin or occur in early childhood. Not realizing, loving parents, family members, or even friends have emotionally wounded their precious child unintentionally by their words or actions. Yes, they are hurt by the people the child loves the most. Many people do not know the power of the spoken word. Words can cut as deep as a knife and leave emotional scars that take years to heal. Some children grow up thinking that it is normal to speak to people in harsh, critical, intimidating, or threatening ways. As they mature, some tend to become "bullies" as teens. As adults, some speak to their own children the same harsh, belittling, yelling way they were accustomed to growing up as a child, believing that it is perfectly normal since they were raised that way. Then again, other children might have a tendency to withdraw inward, becoming more passive as adults. This is exhibited by choosing their words and actions carefully, never trying to offend anyone by speaking in a harsh tone nor in a hurtful manner. They try to avoid being intimidating or inconsiderate to others. They always try to "fix" things—the peacemakers. Unfortunately, many of these same emotionally wounded children become victims again and again, as they seem to have a predisposition throughout life to migrate toward the over-bearing and controlling personalities of people, friends, and even jobs. As this now grown, emotionally wounded person has had a tendency to migrate toward those abusive personalities, this apparent predisposition doesn't stop when it comes time to marry. When choosing a mate and considering marriage, it's almost deja vu, with these wounded people innocently marrying into abusive relationships. They seem to be drawn into the same scenario especially when someone profusely apologizes, promising that the behavior will change. Repeatedly, this wounded adult wants to help "fix" the problem. The cycle of abuse continues and can even escalate to include every type of abuse— until someone finally decides to break the cycle.

This is where my story begins…

I am one of "The Walking Wounded." One day recently, I decided to take a huge step by consulting a counselor after something triggered an emotional melt down resulting in hours of crying, anxiety, and bewilderment. Naturally, I started crying again before I even entered the counselor's office and continued to cry the entire time I was there. Just thinking and talking about my past and all the traumas that I have been through brought back so much pain. I actually thought I was over all of the pain and past emotional wounds—that seemed to be years ago, even another life ago—surely, by now I have been healed of all those scars! I realize that these wounds can no longer be just covered up with bandages. They finally need to be totally exposed so that the healing can be completed.

As a nurse, I know that some physical wounds may seem superficial or just surface wounds, but sometimes they are actually deeper than they seem. Some of these wounds have to be opened up or debrided so that the healing can come from deep within the wound bed. Any physical scars that I have on my body are only superficial, but they can't be compared to my scars which are not visible to the naked eye. These deep, invisible wounds have been cut down to my core where only my Creator can see them. He sees the wounds on my soul and on my spirit, and He is the only one who can heal them. He knows my heart and every wound in it. He knows everyone's heart. And He will judge all of our hearts. Consequently, in order for God to forgive us when we are judged, we have to forgive ourselves and others, even our abusers. We are all human and have all hurt someone (to various degrees) in our lifetime, whether intentionally or unintentionally. We have to choose to forgive, realizing that forgiving does not mean forgetting—Forgiving just means being merciful and releasing any anger or resentment that we have toward a person who has hurt us. We need to give all of our negative feelings to God for Him to deal with those who have hurt us as He deems appropriate.

I have chosen to forgive every person in my lifetime that has harassed me, criticized me, laughed at me, hit me, intimidated me, yelled at me, lied to me or about me, raped me, and even tried to kill me. I forgive every abuser in my life and pray for their healing too. I have come to realize that they have wounds as well which has caused them to behave or react the way that they responded at each moment in our lives. Most importantly, **the first step to <u>my</u>** *total healing* **is** *total forgiveness.*

The new counselor told me that I should write a book with all the things that I have been through over the years. I rejected that idea at first; then, this title came to my mind as I thought about it. Well, this is the beginning of my book—a book of total healing for me and others who have been abused and need miraculous healing. It is about the kind of healing that can only come from God, our Great Physician—our Great Healer. It is a story about my path from brokenness to wholeness.

CHAPTER 2

The Years of Innocence

"Children, obey your parents because you belong to the Lord,
for this is the right thing to do, 'Honor your father and mother'...
and now a word to you fathers. Don't make our children angry
by the way you treat them. Rather, bring them up with the
discipline and instruction approved by the Lord."
Ephesians 6:1-4(NLT)

All children are born with innocence, never having seen blatant evil. They have to be taught what is right and what is wrong. These children learn from birth as their parents lovingly hold them, speaking softly and lovingly to them. They also learn from day one if their parents are not gentle with them or neglect them. These innocent children are like sponges, absorbing everything they come in contact with on a daily basis. They learn through all of their senses—hearing, seeing, feeling, smelling, and tasting. That is one reason that babies want to touch everything they see and put everything in their mouth; it is part of learning. As parents, most of us try to protect our children from harm. We teach them not to touch fire so that they will not get burned. We teach them not to put poison in their mouth. We, as parents, tell children to look with their eyes but don't touch with their hands. We try to protect them from physical injury, but what about any emotional injury? Do parents even realize the harm that is caused by some of their words or actions? Children still learn by everything that they hear and see. These are portals of entry for what is right or wrong. How many times have you heard, even jokingly, "Do what I say, not what I do."? All children learn from <u>everything</u> that is said and <u>everything</u> that is done.

Parents and families are the primary role models for babies and young children initially. Children watch and learn not only the good or positive things that are purposefully taught, but also the bad or negative things that are seen and heard. The sweet, encouraging words that build up a child emotionally or the critical, destructive words that tear down a child emotionally will affect a child. All of these positive and negative behaviors have a cumulative effect on children, whether good or bad. Children often reproduce the behaviors that they learn from parents and families. Their foundation for their own interpersonal relationships is molded during the beginning years of their lives.

Parents need to be careful to lead appropriately by example. We need to realize the effect that our own behaviors have on our children. Are we telling them to "do what we say, but not what we do"? If parents don't want their child to grow up doing something, then they should not expose their child to it. When a parent criticizes or speaks to a child in a demeaning way, that child believes it and learns to treat others that way. If a child is told that he is fat, ugly, stupid, lazy, or "good for nothing", the child believes this, altering his self-esteem. If a parent tells a child that he was not wanted or not loved, even if he says it jokingly, it becomes accepted as truth. Even if a parent fails to tell a child that he is loved or fails to show that love, the child grows up feeling unloved. When a child is always told or shown negative behaviors or even witnesses others treated that way, he begins to think in negative ways. His actions and reactions including his thoughts and comments will mimic what he learned through the years. As parents, most try to protect their children from physical harm, but what about this emotional harm? The emotional development of our children is just as important as their physical development. These emotional traumas, even from early childhood, cause emotional wounds that carry on through their next phases of growth.

This is where my story continues…

I was one of these young, innocent victims. I was the shy, overweight child that was always ignored or picked on as far back as I can remember. I was the middle child of five children in a family that was very concerned about their social life and did not seem to notice that one of their children seemed lost. My mom hugged me and showed affection more than my dad. My dad showed little affection to anyone and never said that he loved me, even though I would hug him and tell him. One grandfather was very verbally and emotionally abusive. My parents were always busy, putting their social needs and financial needs first. My mother was very passive and was controlled financially and emotionally by my father as my father had multiple extramarital affairs, always while claiming to be working. I grew up helping in family businesses as far back as I can remember. I watched as my parents worked together, drank together, and fought together.

I grew up being the one that was afraid of men, especially my abusive grandfather, because he always yelled at me and called me names. Other siblings and cousins adored him, but I just knew that I was afraid of even being around him. One particularly sad memory occurred when I was a small child. He embarrassed me in front of my entire extended family by throwing water on me. I was sitting "Indian-style" in a dress with my panties showing, but I was only a child. The appropriate correction would be to lovingly explain that little girls should not sit like that while wearing a dress—not throw a huge glass of water between my legs for all to see and laugh at me. Neither my parents nor any other adult there defended me as I ran out the room dripping and crying. No one would stand up to that man! I was the one grandchild that was always laughed at when they made all the children dance because it looked so funny with my obesity even as a young child. I was the one who cried whenever I had to stay with my grandparents because of the way that he treated me. Needless to say, that did not help the situation at all, because my grandfather would yell and scream at me even more.

Feelings of insecurity, inadequacy, and low self-esteem started as a small child. I was the family introvert. I later laughed and said that it was because I was the middle child with an older sister and brother and a younger sister and brother. I used to jokingly say that I was never anything special, not the first nor the last. Later, I realized that there actually is something called "middle child syndrome" where these children feel overlooked and starved for attention. Some of these middle children become the peacemakers and over-achievers. Others become the problem-child in the family. However, both types are just wanting or seeking attention. Whichever path they take, the initial cause is the same—a feeling of being unloved due to a perceived lack of parental affection.

These emotional wounds unknowingly inflicted upon me, my siblings, and many other small children like us, greatly affected my emotional health and the foundation for my future interpersonal relationships. The first years of a child's life are like stepping stones to their future and are vital for their future development. I had become the passive peacemaker at an early age and grew into a passive, peacemaking adult. Other siblings were affected in different ways.

All children in a family are affected in some way by abusive and negative characteristics of the family and people that they are in contact with during early childhood. Not surprisingly, out of the five children in my family, four of us became victims of some type of abuse—whether emotional abuse, verbal abuse, physical abuse, sexual abuse and/or adultery, financial abuse, etc. The behaviors that we had learned as children had become acceptable as adults and affected the decisions that we made as we matured. Some of us still suffer the effects of the various abuses in our lives. This is why it is so important that all children from birth are taught positive behaviors in a kind and loving atmosphere for a potential positive outcome to their future relationships and entire lives.

CHAPTER 3

The School Years

"All praise to the God and Father of our Lord Jesus Christ.
He is the source of every mercy and the God who comforts us.
He comforts us in all our troubles so that we can comfort others.
When others are troubled, we will be able to give
them the same comfort that God has given us."
2 Corinthians 1:3-4(NLT)

When a child starts school, his circle of influence, which has basically been mostly family, broadens to include many more people—teachers, students, and other adults. The foundation of his physical, emotional, and spiritual growth has already begun since birth, but he has many more years of development or formation to be continued. Some small children are very outgoing or extroverts. Others are withdrawn or introverts. The emotional development of a young child is already evident once he starts school and interacts with others. The control and protection that a parent has had over a child in their own home diminishes as the child's sphere increases with age. Children mingle with other students from different backgrounds and again learn different behaviors. Many assertive children who were verbally or emotionally abused at home become the students that harass others at school. This is normal behavior for them. They may become the bullies that harass and intimidate others, and often, even the parents do not see a problem in their behavior. Then, many passive children who may be verbally or emotionally abused at home become the victims again at school—the loner child that everyone wants to tease or the child that no one wants to play with. This is also the child that will not report the problem to anyone. He just becomes more and more withdrawn and alone because his ability to form friendships has already been affected in his first few years of life.

These patterns may start in early grade school but continue through high school. Bullying is often accepted by most as "that's just how he or she is." The fact is that it is abuse—emotional, verbal, and even some physical abuse. However, with the increase in school shootings and teen suicides, more attention has been brought to the problem of bullying. Also, with the increase of technology, more and more students have been victims of bullying by being harassed over the internet. The new term is cyber-bullying. It is one thing to be abused at school, but the pain that it causes escalates when it is placed on the internet for all to see and hear. Teachers, parents, and other adults all need to be watching for these signs of abuse. The emotional wounds that are caused by this behavior are detrimental to a child. Again, physical wounds are visible, but these emotional wounds are not visible to the naked eye.

This is where my story continues…

I was the one who cried uncontrollably on my first day of school in the first grade. I was so insecure. My mother just dropped me off at school—not bothering to walk me to my classroom like most parents. Most kids made fun of me and laughed at me at school. Older girls would laugh and pinch my fat cheeks. I remember the entire school laughing at me one day as I was chased around the building. I was the one that even some of my siblings later unknowingly harassed me at home and at school. However, I was always the one that had to give in since I was the quieter or maybe the quitter. I never did like confrontation. I was the peacemaker of the bunch.

Every year, I watched my parents drink, party, and then fight. I cried out to my dad not to leave us as my parents fought about another woman, only to see him get in his truck and leave. I knew at an early age that they were having marital problems. I longed to have my dad hug me and tell me he loved me. However, he was always gone to either work or play. My mother relied on his income to support the five children. I was the child that decided at my young age that it was my responsibility to keep my family together. I was always trying to make peace with everyone and always trying to be perfect so that they would be proud of me. I tried to excel in everything that I did. I went to school every day and mostly sat by myself. I even remember bringing bags of bubble gum to elementary school everyday to give to my supposed friends. It seems that I couldn't even buy a friend.

Then, I never seemed to fit in with any group in high school. I tried to be part of everything possible, but continued to be alone. Multiple times, someone threw slimy green frogs on me in the girl's dressing room. Being overweight, I did not like changing in front of anyone with their snickering, much less running from frogs, half-clothed. Again, everyone got a good laugh at my expense. All through high school, I spent more time alone than anyone. I sat in the library alone day after day when no one wanted to hang out with me. One sibling would complain at school about me and then everyone would turn against me—again. I was bullied again and again and didn't even realize that there was a term for the treatment

I was getting. I was so very lonely that I sat and counted all the tiny holes in the ceiling tiles in the library. On the outside, it looked like I wanted to be there. I was an honor student, so it appeared that I always wanted to study. I was in every sport available and the band so I stayed very busy. All I really wanted were friends. I tried to get involved in everything for companionship. Although there were many teachers, students, and others around me, I felt that I was all alone in the world—totally isolated. No one could see the pain that I was living in. No one even bothered to notice the tears.

CHAPTER 4

Bullying

"So in everything, do to others what you would have them do to you..."
Matthew 7:12(NLT)

Bullying or harassment of others has been happening for decades or even centuries. Bullying and now cyber-bullying are just new terms for the same old word—abuse. Abuse includes intimidation, embarrassing comments, constant criticism, name-calling, humiliating remarks, and sadly, all of these things can be found routinely in schools and on many of these cyber social networks. The comments may seem innocent on the surface to many, but some victims of this abuse realize the underlying meaning or intimidation attached to what is said verbally or written.

The problem seems to still be escalating today with the internet. Thousands of teens are affected by this form of abuse everyday, but it continues to go unnoticed. Their isolation is even more compounded because thousands or even millions of people can potentially see the comments on these cyber social networks. It seems that there are no secrets anymore. Everything gets plastered all over the internet for all to see. People of all ages post where they are, who they are with, what they are thinking, and what they are doing in each moment of the day. There are positive comments posted as well as hurtful, sarcastic, and degrading comments that cause confusion and hurt to innocent victims.

As parents, teachers, and friends, we all need to watch for the signs of anyone who is hurting and reach out to help and comfort those in need. Many teenagers around this country have so much going for them, but live in constant turmoil with the harassment they get by bullies, in person and over the internet. This is happening in public schools, private schools, and social groups. These teens become so distraught that a large number of them commit suicide to escape the abuse. Teens from every social level are affected. Some teens, instead of turning the hurt inward to harm themselves, decide to turn the hurt outward. These are the ones that make the front page of the newspaper when they go on a shooting spree at a school.

Recently, bullying has received much media attention. Teen suicides because of bullying and abuse are now being reported. Previously, school shootings were the only times that bullying at schools were mentioned. Whether a suicide or school shooting, the root causes of both situations were usually the same—some type of abuse. The end results of both situations are horrifically the same—the tragic death of someone's child.

This is where my story continues…

I know how emotionally abused teenagers feel. It happened to me in the 1970's. However, there are many more teens who feel the same way or even worse now. The harassment hurt then, but I can't even imagine how teens that are cyber-bullied feel today.

Most of my life had been affected by bullying. My parents never paid attention to the treatment that I received at home from one of my own siblings. Then, this treatment would follow me to school where everyone at school would turn against me, as complaints from home followed me to school. I was usually trying to be the good, obedient child while my sibling tried to follow what everyone did at school, despite my parent's objections. If my parents found out about any of us breaking a parental rule, I was blamed for tattling even if I was innocent. My sibling was so full of anger and resentment which was probably the result of some kind of unknown abuse as well during our early childhood. Unfortunately, I was the recipient of most of the wrath that occurred. When I did try to complain about the harassing treatment that I was receiving, I was always told to just let them have their way. I was always told to give in since I was older. I quickly learned even as a child to never complain about any harassing or abusive treatment. I had learned to just live with it, no matter how bad the harassment increased. Neither my parents nor my other family members saw the treatment that I received most days under the same roof. I just learned after all those years to suffer in silence.

A more recent example of bullying with horrific consequences occurred in my life this past year. Another teenager decided that she could no longer suffer in silence. She was a victim of emotional abuse and cyber-bullying. She was the granddaughter of a dear friend of mine who has supported me and my children throughout our ordeal with abuse. She was being bullied at school and cyber-bullied. This young teenager was one of the most beautiful girls in her school. She was also one of the sweetest and kindest girls that anyone could meet. I know this because I had known her since she was born. I had watched her grow up with her father and his family into a beautiful young lady. However, the deep wounds of her past were not visible to the naked eye.

She was born into one of the wealthiest families in the area, a family that could have provided everything she needed. Unfortunately, they could not heal the wounds of abandonment caused by her birth mother. She was already wounded, but then she began being bullied at school. Her family moved her to a different school, but that did not stop the harassment. The cyber-bullying continued everywhere she went. This family could have moved her anywhere in the country or the world to protect her, and they would have if they had known the extent of the problem. Money was not a concern. This young girl had more options than the majority of teens that are harassed. She could have started a new life somewhere, free of harassment. However, this wounded child could not see that she had multiple options through all the pain she was experiencing. She suffered in silence, not letting her family know the extent of the problems she was experiencing. Then one day, surprisingly and tragically, she ended her own life with a gun.

More attention needs to be brought to the root problem of bullying which is abuse. Children are experiencing inappropriate or negative behaviors at home, on television, and also at schools which may cause emotional wounds. Many of these children suffer in silence. Some of these children, in an effort to "fit in" with others or to avoid being bullied themselves, join together to harass someone else. The harassment continues until someone gets hurt. It is time to stop justifying it as just normal adolescent behavior and quit ignoring it. Homes and schools should be a place of protection and safety, not abuse. We should all just treat others the way that we want to be treated.

CHAPTER 5

Through the Looking Glass

"The thief does not come except to steal, and to kill, and to destroy.
I have come that they may have life and that
they may have it more abundantly."
John 10:10(NKJV)

A person's life choices are affected by his life experiences. To a young adult who has been wounded by any abuse through the years, his perception of things can be distorted. If a person looks at an item or situation through rose-colored glasses, it looks all rose-colored. When another person looks at the same item or situation through dirty glasses, everything looks dirty. Their reception of actions or words is altered as a result of the trauma in their life affecting the way that they interpret or perceive various things.

What many abused people believe as truths may in fact be untruths. Their God-given talents may be hindered because of their self-perception. The decisions that they make are affected by the wounds they have from the type of abuse that they experienced. Their choices of careers can be affected because their self-esteem is affected. Their choice of life partners can be affected. Their treatment of future children can be affected. It is not uncommon for a person who was abused as a child to turn around and abuse their own children. They believe that this is normal behavior. Some passive abused adults tend to choose spouses that are abusive. This may be what their passive parent did also. Some sexually abused children may become promiscuous, or turn to same-sex relationships, or become child molesters themselves. Many decisions that are made in a lifetime are affected by the wounds that may have occurred during their developmental years.

The Bible talks about people dying for lack of knowledge. There are many people who feel like they are dying on the inside. They are hurting from the wounds of their youth caused by actions or words that were spoken to them. People do not know the power of the spoken word where life or death is spoken into someone's life. We have to open our eyes and our hearts to reach out to the hurting and speak "life" back into them. We have to educate people about abuse. It is not just the visibly bruised and beaten that are injured. There are many more with invisible wounds from abuse that are also injured and need help to get back on the path that God has planned for them and reach their full potential.

This is where my story continues again…

I, as a young teenager, was an honor student in the top of my class. I was involved in almost everything possible for girls in our school, except cheerleading. I was overweight and would never get into those skimpy cheerleading outfits. I was on the basketball team and even won the MVP award as well as many other awards by the end of my senior year. I was on the volleyball team. I played an instrument in the band and won many awards through the years. I won many academic awards for my scholastic achievements. I was on the student council and actively involved in my school's academic and athletic events. I graduated as the Valedictorian of my class. I always gave 100% in everything that I attempted. However, with all of my achievements, the initial thought would be that I appear to be very successful and popular. Amazingly, all that I wanted to do was get away from that small town where everyone had teased me or harassed me. All I could think of was to get away from everyone that hated me, and I thought that almost everyone hated me. My self-esteem was so low that I couldn't picture myself as having any friends or being successful. I was looking through hurt eyes. My vision was distorted by the events in my life.

I spent many, many days sitting alone in the library or on the school grounds. I remembered walking up to groups only to see them all get up and walk away. I remembered the snide comments that were muttered under their breaths. I remembered always getting laughed at as ugly comments were made. I even remembered the embarrassing things like being chased as a child around the school in the first grade by a boy trying to kiss me while the entire student population watched and laughed…especially after I slipped in the mud in a dress that my mother always made me wear. I remembered being mocked because my mother made me wear home-made clothes (especially since they were clothes that my grandmother would have worn). I remembered being harassed about my weight constantly. I also remembered standing up for myself once and getting hit in the elbow with a baton so hard that my arm just hung lifeless, paralyzed for hours. I remembered being threatened with a knife because I was a straight "A" student. I kept all of these things bottled up inside and always protected the person that hurt me. I remembered more of the bad stuff than the good stuff. I just wanted to get away from everyone who had ever hurt me.

Then, as a lonely teenager, I went off to college to "start a new life". However, even in college, I was a quiet, shy teenager and continued with few friends. My self-esteem was so low that I had trouble making friends. I was not the bubbly, fun-loving girl that everyone wanted to be with. My ability to develop interpersonal relationships had been negatively affected by all the years of emotional and verbal abuse and the many feelings of being unwanted and unloved.

Then, I met this guy one weekend. He was introduced to me by a cousin. He was **so** nice to me. He told me that he had always wanted to meet me. He told me that he had heard all about me through mutual friends and some family. In fact, he was best friends with this cousin and another close family friend. He knew all about my high school years, had read my graduation speech, and had even seen my baby pictures. He even told me, **"I finally get to meet you!"** He also told me that he had always heard that I was the nicest girl that anyone could ever meet. Wow! I was totally "blown away"! I was a shy young girl, who never had much self-esteem, and right then, I was hearing all of these compliments from a stranger. He was saying things that no one had ever said to me. He was obviously excited to meet me! The excitement that I felt was indescribable! Someone was finally interested in me!

Unfortunately, I fell for it like bait in a trap. I was so hungry for friendship, attention, companionship, and love after years of being lonely and feeling unloved, that I couldn't even see the warning signs. I dated this guy for two years, mostly long-distance and seeing each other on weekends when I was home from college. I either didn't see it or totally ignored his obvious low self-esteem and issues with anger, resentment, etc. I received many warnings from family and friends that he was lying and deceiving me, and that he was using me for financial gain. The warning signs increased including outbursts and excessive alcohol consumption. The smoking he promised he stopped actually continued… just in secret. The outbursts of anger were followed by remorse and promises that it won't happen again. The unhidden abusive behaviors of his parents were followed by comments that he would never act like his parents. The behaviors that I told him that I did not like were hidden from me. He pretended to be someone that he wasn't. Unfortunately, I fell in love for the first time. I was the girl who thought that I would be alone forever and was actually in love with someone, or someone that I thought that he was. I could not see the truth. I could not see that I was being manipulated. My decisions were affected by the wounds that I had from the time that I was a young child. I had been trained to never complain. I had been trained to always accept everything in silence. Someone that I would have run from if I had been emotionally healthy and able to see clearly had now became my future husband.

CHAPTER 6
Newlyweds

"And you husbands must love your wives, with the same love Christ showed the church."
Ephesians 5:25(NLT)

There are stages of abuse—initially, the abuser hides his true self. It is like a game to set boundaries. He pretends to be someone that he is not. He is very careful not to offend his partner and learns how far he can push the limits. They are learning about each other, but the abuser is literally scoping out his prey while hiding basic truths about himself. But this stage only lasts so long. Gradually, his anger and frustration begin showing more and more. That short fuse that he has gets lit and intensifies until he blows up. His fuse gets shorter and shorter with more frequent explosions. Finally, his true self is revealed. His dominance over his victim gets established. He makes it known who makes the decisions and who is in charge.

Power and control are the name of the game that he plays. He verbally beats his victim down to total submission usually before the physical and sexual assaults or violence ever occurs. The verbal and emotional abuse becomes so common that it is accepted as normal behavior. The victim does not even realize anymore what is happening. Constant criticism, name-calling, humiliating comments, as well as threatening comments shape their relationship. What was left of the self-esteem and identity as a separate person is destroyed.

The victim is always apologizing for things that they have not even done. They are the peacekeeper or peacemaker and always trying to please their mate. They lose any self confidence that they may have had. They live in constant fear of doing something or saying something that will cause their abuser to explode again. However, sometimes it doesn't take much to set off an abuser. These explosive fuses are even shorter when alcohol is involved. Alcohol lowers a person's inhibitions when they are intoxicated, so imagine the volatility of that situation when considering an abuser. Some victims are even just sleeping when an attack occurs. After the explosion occurs, then the abuser is remorseful again but rarely apologizes. It is the honeymoon phase again where the victim is treated so kindly. This period of asking forgiveness and remorse are actually methods of manipulation that the abuser uses to keep control over his victims. Many promises occur in this phase but most fail to come true. Broken promises are actually another aspect of abuse. It abuses the trust that the victim has in the spouse. The victim clings to the hope that the person that they love, despite being an abuser or batterer, will change. In most cases, the abuser doesn't feel that he has even done anything wrong. He always blames the victim for making him upset or angry or making him lose his temper. He claims it is the victim's fault when he gets mad and hits a wall with his fist or throws an object in anger. The abuser also will constantly put his victim down in front of other people—criticizing everything, calling them stupid or other put-downs, just to boast his own self. To most, he is a very nice guy at first.

It is only after more time is spent with the abuser and his victim that his guard is down and more of his true personality is revealed to others.

Most abusers are master manipulators and deceivers. They can manipulate many situations, but the truth will eventually be exposed because they can't always hide their feelings of resentment, frustration, and anger. The next problem becomes one of people not wanting to get involved. Many people may hear or see the abuse, but they do not want to offend anyone to speak up. They may also fear retaliation from the abuser himself. Many family members may see what is happening, but most abusers alienate the victim from her families. The victim may have been repeatedly warned about the abuser by family members so they feel that they have no one to turn to—they feel all alone. There is an old saying that, "You have made your bed; now lie in it." It refers to making a mistake, but now you have to live with the consequences. Many women may have been warned by family and then told, "Don't come running back to me when it happens." Unfortunately, these women were just so hungry for companionship and love that they were targets for these manipulative, abusive men.

This is where my story continues again…

Yes, I was one of these women. Very low self esteem and feeling unloved from my childhood led to very poor decision making as an adult. I ignored all the warnings from my family and friends. I could not see through the deceitful behavior and even when I could, I chose to ignore it. When he told me that he used to watch me from a distance while I visited a friend's house, I thought it was so cute. I was probably about twelve years old then. When he told me that he used to watch me play tennis on the local tennis courts when I was a young teenager, I thought that was so awesome. He knew all about me from family and friends. He had seen my pictures as I grew up, and he never told me that I was fat or ugly at that time. Then, he was always saying that I was so cute and so sweet. The big warning sign that I failed to realize was that he didn't have enough self-esteem or think enough about himself to come to introduce himself to me—and that happened many years before we actually met.

When I think about that man watching me years ago from a distance, I now realize that there is a term for it. It is called **"stalking,"** and it is a pattern of behavior in an abusive relationship. It is where someone watches and waits for a person to harass or pursue them with unwanted or obsessive attention. (Wikipedia.org) He had watched me from afar for seven or eight years, but he never stood where I even noticed him at the time. Many years later after we were married, I remembered seeing a young boy on a bicycle watching my sister and I and a friend while we played croquet in the friend's backyard. This friend of mine happened to be the same friend that told my ex-husband when he was a teenager that I was the nicest person that anyone could ever meet and that he was not good enough to even meet me. When I remembered that young boy watching from the next block, I asked him about that day many years before. He acknowledged that it was him on the bike and that he had been watching me even then. He was waiting for the day that he could meet me.

We started dating when we met. We were going to bars and drinking. Within weeks, he was already saying that he loved me. Those words were so special to hear. Those were words that I had never heard before at that time. My family rarely told each other that they loved each other. (I was 26 years old the first time that I heard my father tell me that he loved me.) Within a few months, he had already proposed. He told me that he loved me and wanted to marry me and spend the rest of his life with me. My heart melted. He gave me an engagement ring, and I was feeling things that I had never felt before. Someone loved me!! I immediately accepted his marriage proposal, not really knowing this man, but I gave my heart to him. We planned to marry after I finished college. He kept telling me that if I truly loved him, I would let him make love to me. That should have been another warning sign.

We continued to date as I went to college. We only saw each other on weekends, and we were usually drinking with friends. My perception of things was already dulled by my low self-esteem, and the excessive alcohol only dulled my vision more. He called me almost every day and said that he loved me. He sent me roses frequently. He was always saying that he would never be like his family, especially abusive like his father was to him. Unfortunately, I believed him. I spent many hours with his family while they were drinking, yelling, fussing, cussing, complaining, etc. I even commented that his dad never had anything nice to say to anyone. His mother was nicer, but they were always cursing and fighting, always verbally abusive and even physically at times. He promised that he would never behave that way. His father was a heavy drinker and always angry. In fact, he described his father as the town drunk.

His own true personality revealed itself more and more, but by that time, I was deeply in love with him and had finally given myself totally to him. I had given a part of myself to my future husband that I could never get back. Even though we were drinking and getting drunk frequently together on weekends, I believed that he would change when we would officially get married and have more responsibilities. I felt in my heart that we were already man and wife—for better or for worse. We had already pledged our everlasting love to each other and consummated a marriage that had not yet occurred. That was probably the biggest mistake that I made in my entire life. I may have felt that I could have walked away from the relationship then, but I had given him a part of myself already. We already had a soul tie. I had been raised with parents drinking and was trained to never complain as my mother always gave in to my father's requests. But I had also been raised basically by my mother believing that a girl should save herself for her wedding night. I had a tremendous amount of guilt about that but had justified it by thinking that we were engaged and planning to marry soon.

One day while I was away at college, my fiancé and my mother actually set the wedding date—then they both called me to tell me when we were getting married. I was already having concerns, but the wedding arrangements had been put in motion and I had already given myself to him. I could not back out now. Unfortunately, he lost his job a few months before the wedding. He was living with his sister, and his behavior deteriorated when he was unemployed. The drinking and abusive words increased when he lost his job before our planned wedding. His feelings of insecurity and inadequacy from his youth compounded his feelings of frustration and resentment with no income as an adult. The wedding plans were in progress, and I had dedicated my life to this man. I felt that everything would work out ok. I did not mind supporting us. I was a hard worker and had worked most of my life in our family businesses. I did not realize the reality of the world that I was about to become part of with this marriage.

He got a job right before we got married but needless to say, we started out with bare minimum. I just knew that I had to get away from my previous life where there was so much hurt. Even during our wedding reception, an invited guest came up to me and laughingly said that he never thought that I would get married. I was laughed at even on the day that was supposed to be the happiest day of my life. My wedding dress was not the most beautiful one that I could find—it was the only one that I could find to fit me. My own father laughed at me during the wedding reception because I could not dance with a partner leading me. I was never taught. No one ever wanted to dance with me. I was even embarrassed at my own wedding reception! I moved several hours away from my family to be with my husband.

We were starting a new life together. I just knew that we would be married "happily ever-after," and that as a team, we could work anything out. What I did not count on was his constant verbal and emotional abuse that was tearing me down. We had seen each other on weekends while I was in college, but it was totally different living with someone. I was constantly being criticized. I was trying to be a good wife but could not do anything right. Meals lovingly prepared the way that my mother had taught me were followed by outbursts of anger because they were "trash" and "not fit for a dog." I didn't cook the way his mother did. I didn't clean the way his mother did. Any little thing would set him off on a rampage of cussing and fussing. I kept trying to please him, but he kept humiliating me, criticizing me, and embarrassing me with all of these sarcastic, negative comments about everything that I did. He repeatedly did this in front of his family and our friends. However, he was always on his best behavior in front of my family. I could not call my family because they had warned me. I did not want them to know that everything was not perfect.

Then, just a few months after our marriage, the big explosion occurred. It was the first time that I experienced the wrath of his violence. I was off of work that day and spent the day cooking and cleaning for a romantic evening with my newlywed husband. The candles were lit when he got home from work, and I lovingly met him at the door. Big mistake!!! He had had a bad day at work. He exploded in anger! He grabbed me, screamed at me, and pushed me into the bedroom. I was crying and yelling **"NO,"** and that I was **"sorry,"** and that I would **"never do it again,"** and to **"please stop"** as he angrily threw me onto the bed, tearing my clothes and his clothes off. He was yelling at me that he was going to **"give it to me!"** My newlywed husband, the man that I loved, was in the process of trying to rape me as I was screaming and struggling for him to stop. He was violently screaming and cursing in anger.

While all of this was happening, his sister walked into our house and stopped him. I was devastated and in shock! I curled up in a ball and cried like a baby. Naturally, everything was my fault. I had caused him to get angry. Sadly, his sister agreed with him. That was the day that I realized that I had married what seemed to be a "Dr. Jekyll and Mr. Hyde." His temperament could change in a split second. I felt so trapped! I had just gotten married despite many warnings, just moved away from my family, just bought a mobile home, and just started a brand new job. I could not call anyone. I could not just leave my new job and house. I could not even tell anyone, because that would only make him even angrier. That explosive day was the day that I started crying out to God—to help me, to save me, to forgive me! I prayed for forgiveness for every mistake that I had ever made in my entire lifetime, including giving myself to that man before marriage and then marrying that violent man. I knew in my heart that God had a better plan for my life. I prayed for my husband to change. Hour after hour, night after night, month after month, I would lie on the very edge of the bed, secretly crying and praying to God and trying to avoid even touching him. I did not want him to think that I was making any romantic gestures toward him. I was terrified that he would hurt me again. I couldn't even let him hear me cry because he would start yelling at me. I was terrified of his volatile behavior. He had sexually assaulted me, but I was made to feel that it was my fault. I had already felt guilty, but now it was multiplied. He had terrorized me and traumatized me, but I could tell no one. I was so confused and hurt. I kept thinking and wondering if this is what marriage was supposed to be. I kept blaming myself for giving myself to him while engaged— maybe his violence would have showed up sooner, and I would have run. Did he have the right to do that to me since we were married? Where did I go wrong? Why didn't I see his violent temper or even potential for violence before?

Many people felt that spousal rape was not really rape, and sexual assault was nonexistent if a couple was married. I had heard the debates that the man had the right to take "it" any way and any time he wanted it from his wife—she was his property. This is not right! Every woman has a right to say NO!!!

The Bible says that husbands and wives should submit to each other and love each other, not abuse each other. I was so wounded before this attack, but then I was even more wounded—emotionally and sexually. It was definitely not love, but I could not describe how I felt. I was in shock. I knew that it was an act of violence. How could someone who supposedly loves a person do something like that to her? He had stolen something from me that could never be replaced. I had given him my virginity, but he stole my innocence. It was like I would never totally feel safe again. I had witnessed a level of violence that I had only heard about or seen in movies. From that moment on, I tried to only move when he told me to move and speak when he told me to speak. I had become his toy—he played with me when he wanted and put me on the shelf when he was through. He was now basically in total control of me.

CHAPTER 7

Marriage

"Teach your children to choose the right path, and when
they are older, they will remain upon it."
Proverbs 22:6 (NLT)

Abuse always cycles around the various stages. The stages of abuse continue from tension building to explosive to another honeymoon phase. The stages may skip back and forth with various lengths between the stages. Abuse is also composed of different types, but they are all still abuse: emotional, verbal, physical, sexual, spiritual, and financial. The victim endures these abuses day by day, accepting them as normal behavior. Her self-esteem gets lower and lower. Her self-confidence is dwindling daily. She gets more nervous and fearful. She gets more apologetic. When she does try to do something for herself, it only opens it up for more harassment and accusations. The more irritable the abuser is, the more the victim is on guard, waiting for another attack.

The victim gets blamed for everything day in and day out and eventually she starts believing that everything that happens is her fault. She even gets afraid to speak at times for fear that he will get angry. She actually begins to think that she may be crazy since she hears it so much. Things that she knows in her heart that she did not do or say, she is accused of anyway. She starts thinking that maybe she did do it or say it and doesn't remember. He has told her that she is crazy or lazy so often that she begins to think that maybe she really is crazy or lazy. She gets reluctant to even make a decision on her own fearing his reaction.

The lack of self-confidence and severe insecurity that the victim had as a child which led to her wrong choice in a mate is growing. She has no self-esteem left. She is more withdrawn, even fearful to participate in idle conversation in case she says something to upset him. She doesn't realize that the words that she mispronounces or the words that she can't remember correctly are because of the stress and intense fear of saying something wrong. She gets harassed for the words that she speaks and makes more mistakes as she worries about what she is saying. That even adds to the fear that something is wrong with her. The abuser constantly intimidates her, harasses her, and degrades her which puts her in a state of fear, never knowing when the next explosion is going to occur again.

Then, when children are born, most anger regarding the children is directed at the wife or victim. When the abuser is tired, more abuse occurs. When the child cries, more abuse occurs. When the abuser gets angry at the child, he whips the child harder than he should. The children are starting to be called degrading names and criticized. The verbal, emotional, and physical abuse begins for the children. The children grow up in this atmosphere of abuse, and the cycle continues with their emotional well-being in jeopardy. Whatever they were exposed to as children becomes acceptable to them. The wife and children are now both victims. But, how does a victim protect her own children from being victims, especially when she is a victim herself? What is the turning point? How can the cycle of abuse be stopped? The victim still feels all alone. She is isolated. But, now she has children to worry about. Where does she turn to? Who can she talk to? Who can help?

This is where my story continues again...

The first year of our marriage was an absolute nightmare. He was drinking every day. On weekends, we would go "party" with his friends back home, getting drunk and rowdy. There was one weekend that he and his buddies were "tearing up" a new 4-wheel drive truck in the mud that he had just bought, even though there was nothing wrong with his previous truck. The truck, brand new, had already had to have repairs to the engine or transmission from his irresponsible use of the vehicle. I tried to tell him, in front of the other men, to be careful since it was new. He got very angry and proceeded to attack me verbally with yelling and screaming and with multiple curse words. He called me horrible names that no one had ever called me before. I got angry and slapped him. Oh, BIG mistake!!! He hit me in the face so hard that I was thrown off balance; my glasses cut my face, and they flew to the ground broken. I was crying and shaking uncontrollably. Our female friends gathered around me as I cried, holding me. They told him that he should not have hit me so hard, but it was my entire fault according to him and the other drunken men. I had slapped him first!

I had responded for the first time in anger and lashed back at him. It was like we had been having a power struggle in our marriage that climaxed at that moment. He would always win. He had just taught me another valuable lesson. He was much stronger than me. That little slap that I gave him just angered him more. He hurt me as he overpowered me with his brute force. He continued to yell and scream at me as our male friends struggled to hold him and get him under control. He later said that he had to knock some sense into me. I had witnessed what happened if I would get angry and try to defend myself or take up for myself. I had learned again to **never** fight back. I just would continue to take the abuse silently. I was repeatedly told that it was entirely my fault, and I truly felt guilty and remorseful for hitting him. I apologized many, many times. However, I had witnessed his total loss of control again when he got angry. It was a level of anger and violence that terrified me. It had taken several men to hold him away from me and to get him calmed down. What if I had been alone with him? What had I done? I was in shock again and could not believe that I had opened a door to potential violence by marrying this person that I loved. I knew that I was wrong for what I did and repeatedly apologized. However, I had again witnessed that he was uncontrollable when he got angry, especially if he was intoxicated.

The first year was followed by years of emotional rollercoaster rides. Yes, we did have some good times, but there were many, many bad times. After that big fight, we stopped going back home every possible weekend to be with his friends where drinking and getting drunk were a certainty. We did try to spend more time together and more time with his family that we lived near. The fussing, cussing, yelling, screaming at me was overwhelming at times. The drinking was excessive at times. The negativity was smothering. Nothing was ever good enough. I just kept trying but never succeeding to please him. He had a control over me, and I would finally just give in to whatever he wanted. I believed that marriage was supposed to be 50-50, and I tried to communicate and compromise for everything from financial planning to planning parenthood. He always said that I was trying to control everything, but somehow I always gave in to what he wanted to keep the peace. I had learned to never lash back in anger. I would be like the mouse that ran away to hide when he was angry. I would withdraw within myself as if I had a secret hiding place. I always had a deep down fear that he would become violent again. He had already taught me a couple of lessons.

The initial turning point to give me courage to change something was with my first pregnancy. The day that I found out that I was pregnant, I was so excited! I could not wait to tell my husband that we were having our first child. I excitedly called him at his co-worker's house to give him the good news. It was followed by the response that we would talk about it at home. I could hear the anger in his voice. Oh, no! Not a good response.

My excitement was beat down; as I was verbally and emotionally beat down once we both got home. He was yelling and screaming at me for getting pregnant. We had been married for almost 6 years. I had just lost a lot of weight and then got pregnant. He had been harassing me for losing weight and accusing me of trying to impress other men. I had lost weight for health reasons. I had been out of work twice on worker's compensation with back injuries while he wasn't working. My blood pressure was high. I was stressed, but I kept pushing myself to get back to work. He was not working, and I needed to support my husband. I had never looked at another man! I loved my husband. I had supported him when he quit work to go to school two years before after his father died. In fact, he was still not working when I got pregnant. I was so excited that we were going to have a baby! We had talked about children and had planned to have children, and now I was finally pregnant. I just cried like a baby with joy knowing that I had our child growing inside of me. I could not understand his response—why he was angry! He had always said that he wanted children. I just figured it was that he was never happy about anything that I had done anyway, not even getting pregnant with our first child.

When I got pregnant, I knew that something had to change in our behavior. I boldly made the announcement that **"God gives you children**

to raise the way He wants them raised." I announced that I would no longer drink alcoholic beverages, and boldly stated that **"children learn by example and I planned to teach them by example."** I quit drinking for the health of my baby, but I continued abstaining from alcohol even after he was born. I didn't smoke and always hated the smell. I quit all cursing even though I rarely did compared to his family who used curse words in almost every sentence. I tried to be the perfect wife and mother.

I prayed for my unborn child and repeatedly begged God to not let my child be like his father. I was still very naïve about what was really going on. I always tried to do what was right. I was 7 months pregnant with our first child the first time that I remember him threatening to leave me. He was yelling and cursing at me, calling me fat, ugly, lazy, and many other degrading words. He wanted to move into a rent house next door to his sister, despite the fact that we had a mobile home that was just paid off and had planned to save money to build a house. He had just returned to work after two years of me supporting him while he went to school; consequently, we had not been able to save any money. I was hoping that now that he was back at work, we could possibly start saving for our future. But he was very angry because I was pregnant. I kept trying to reason with him, but he told me that he was renting that house—with or without me. He told me that I could just stay in the mobile home with my baby because he was moving out!

He always made impulsive decisions with little thought into conse-quences and then got angry when I tried to reason with him. He would then blame me for the results of his own impulsiveness. He could not look past his immediate desires. I was his scapegoat whom he blamed for every-thing. We ended up renting that house for a year before we could purchase it. Meanwhile, we paid rent for a mobile home slot in a trailer park for a year before we could sell it, but only after having to spend more money on repairs for a water leak that went unnoticed because the house was empty for so long.

After the birth of our first child, I continued to not drink or "party" anymore. I continued to try to teach by example through the birth of all 3 of our children, each 3 years apart. I kept trying to protect them from the fussing, cussing, alcohol, and many inappropriate things for children to witness. I vividly remember grabbing my children as toddlers from my in-laws next door as they gave them alcohol and put cigarettes in their mouths as my husband laughed in agreement. They had all been allowed to drink and smoke at young ages and thought that it was cute for a young child to do the same. I repeatedly announced that my children will not drink and smoke! I would take my children home immediately, removing them from the situation, then hear the yelling and screaming that followed. My husband had been drinking and smoking since he was thirteen years old, and he did not see a problem with it. Then, I would continue to pray that my children would not be like their father and his family. They did not even see what was wrong in their behavior. Their parents were abusive to them and allowed them to drink, smoke, curse and fight. I wanted better for my children but kept praying for God to heal our marriage and protect my children. I wanted us to be a normal family.

I continued to be the target for most of the abuse, but my children were experiencing it as well. I took on the role of the protector, but I could not protect them from the ones who were emotionally and verbally abusing me while living in that situation. We were still hours away from my family, so his family members were the primary relatives that my children knew and loved. As my children got older, they were witnessing more and more inappropriate behavior, including drug addictions and sexual behaviors, in the family and elsewhere. I could not even see how bad the abuse was until I was out of it. Also, it was not until I was out of the situation that many old friends started coming forward and being truthful about backing out of our lives. The married couple who were our neighbors and spent time with us as our families grew had suddenly become too busy to socialize with us. The real reason was hid for years. They saw the abuse and that I was too beat down to see it. They saw the erratic behavior in my husband as well as in our entire family. They heard the cursing, saw the drunkenness, and saw that the kids and I amazingly thought it was normal. They did not want their children exposed to this behavior and abuse. They were protecting their children by avoiding us.

As my children were growing up, I continued to pray that the cycle of abuse and alcoholism would be broken from my children. I repeatedly told my children from the time that they were little that they were **"held to a higher standard of behavior"** and were **"not allowed to curse and do the things that others did."** I would not allow them to say mean things to people or even about people. They were not allowed to say even seemingly simple things that just did not sound right or sounded harsh. I did not want them to use the word "hate." I told them that this word was too strong and hurt people. I told them that there was too much hate in this world, and we had to be different. Hate sounded like a mean word so we had to avoid it. I taught them that it was ok to say that you did not like something like broccoli, but not to even say that they hated it. It was ok to say that you did not like something that someone did or said but never to say that you hated that person. I would not even allow them to use any vulgar word regarding feces because it sounded like a curse word. It did not matter that no one even thought of it as a curse word. I did not allow them to use racially degrading words or to "pick" on anyone. I tried to teach them all to treat people with love and respect. Deep down, I knew that I did not want them hurting anyone like I had been hurt.

This was about the time that **"WWJD"** was popular. I repeatedly told my children that for all decisions that they made, they needed to consider **"What would Jesus do?"** I told them that they were all held to a higher standard of behavior and could not act like others. I knew deep down that I had really messed up and still felt guilty by not considering this when I was younger. I wanted better for my children. I never wanted them to feel that they had to marry someone. I witnessed my own parents drink and go to parties, so drinking was no big problem when I was younger. I did not see them drunk, but I watched them behave in ways that did not seem appropriate for children. I was raised with the **"Do what I say, but not what I do"** mentality. The inappropriate behaviors that I witnessed as a child were nothing compared to what my kids and I witnessed in my spouse's family. They had absolutely no inhibitions, especially when they were intoxicated, which was frequently. Sexual comments, sexual exhibits, drug usage, and inappropriate nicknames were almost daily occurrences. Imagine teaching a child to call his own grandmother, Big Pu_ _y (and it's not puppy) or being in a store and hearing that yelled across the store. There was no respect for themselves or each other. I strongly believed that I had to teach my children the importance of treating <u>everyone with respect</u>. I also believed that I had to fight to stop the cycle of alcoholism and abuse that plagued our families, especially their dad's family. I did not want my children to be alcoholics or abusive to anyone.

I kept trying to teach our children right from wrong, but my standards were being broken down from the harassment that I constantly received. Years later, we had even started going to Bourbon Street as a family, where my children were seeing things that they should not have been exposed to there. I had even restarted drinking "frozen drinks" like pina coladas with ice cream. Through the years, I had been repeatedly told that I was boring, hard-headed, etc. since I had not been drinking since the birth of our first child. I had finally given in to his demands. I made sure that I limited it, never getting drunk on those "desert-like" drinks in the presence of our children. However, I was allowing a door to open with alcohol that I had said that I would never do. I just kept telling my children that they were not allowed to act like the behaviors that they saw. I did not realize that I was being broken down into that parental pattern of "Do what I say, but not what I do" instead of the "teaching by example" pattern that I had used since my children were born.

The Bible says to **"treat people the way you want to be treated."** I told my children that if they wanted people to be nice to them, then they had to be nice the other people. They were raised saying "yes ma'm, no ma'm, yes sir, no sir." I also believed that I had to be the example for my children especially considering that they saw the exact opposite in our own household. They were raised with two opposite personalities—one with anger and resentment and the other with kindness and gentleness. I had been told that their dad "had no fuse" and that I had a fuse that went for miles and miles. I very seldom got angry. I had seen what acting out in anger had caused me. I was told though that I was too strict sometimes, but I just felt in my heart that I could not waiver in my teaching. I did not harshly spank my children like their father. I truly believed in just telling them right from wrong, and I just kept praying that God would keep them on the right path. I was verbally and emotionally abused even more for my parenting beliefs and was frequently told that I was absolutely crazy.

I did not know where these strong feelings about teaching my children by example came from at the time. I actually thought that I had turned out ok despite my parents partying and drinking on weekends. However, I could not deny what was in my heart regarding my children being held to a higher standard of behavior. I had no idea at the time who they were to become as followers of Christ. I just now know that God has told us that He has big plans for them. I didn't even realize that God had placed this in my heart. I just kept praying and walking through the life that I had chosen. I prayed for my family—for my husband to change and for my children to become the people that God wanted them to be. I did not want them making the same mistakes that I had made or for them to hurt people the way that I had been hurt. Amazingly, God answered most of my prayers but not in the way that I expected it.

"For I know the plans that I have for you," says the Lord. "They are plans for good, not for disaster, to give you a future and a hope." Jeremiah 29:11(NLT)

CHAPTER 8

Wounds

"I command you— be strong and courageous! Do not be afraid or discouraged. For the Lord your God is with you wherever you go."
Joshua 1:9 (NLT)

Many abusers are so dissatisfied with themselves and life that they are always searching for something else—something new to add excitement to their lives. They are so miserable that they are always looking for something to do or somewhere to go or just anything to add excitement. Then, the victim still gets the blame for any lack of money or him being tired or anything that he feels fit to yell about. The abuser controls everything. If she gets off work at 4pm, he may be calling by 4:05 to ask why she is not home yet. If she goes to the store, he watches the clock for her to return, and then yells if she is a few minutes late. If she avoids him sexually, he yells and complains that she must not love him because she doesn't make the first move. He seems to be always looking for reasons to yell and turns many things around for his benefit. He may do something and then accuse her of doing it. The majority of the time, it is because he has already done it. He can do anything or go anyplace. The chances are that if the abuser accuses his spouse of looking at other men, it is probably because he has looked at other women. If the abuser accuses his innocent spouse of having sex with someone else, the chances are that he has already had an affair with someone else. The Bible says that **"Out of the abundance of the heart, the mouth speaks."** That means that what is in someone's heart is really what comes out of their mouth. If someone is always calling a person fat, then says that he is joking, the chances are that he really is not joking and believes that they are fat. It's like a jab with a knife that cuts down to the soul. The constant criticism tears down the victim emotionally. The accusations of infidelity may even be made in a joking manner, but the concern is the root cause of the accusations. The anger, resentment, frustration, lust, sexual immorality and all other inappropriate feelings within a person are exhibited as they act on these feelings. As the abuser acts out in anger to verbally, emotionally, physically, and sexually assault the victim, he may also act on his lust and sexual inappropriate behaviors with others. This unfaithfulness in his marriage is actually another form of abuse—abusing trust. The more that the abuser can successfully hide this unfaithfulness from his spouse, the more that he continues to be unfaithful. Also, as other women continue to respond positively to his advances, the more the boundaries of infidelity are pushed back for more inappropriate behavior with others. Just like the phases of abuse, infidelity starts out "testing the waters" then progresses. Again, the abuser or adulterer is looking for an excitement that he feels that he doesn't have with his spouse. It is that desire for adventure, for secret pleasures, and for something new and exciting that drives his behaviors. Unfortunately, this endangers the innocent spouse for more deep wounds of all kinds.

Infidelity causes more wounds to the victim's heart and soul. Besides the wounds of abuse, the wounds of infidelity can go even deeper. Infidelity is a type of rejection which is a major source of hurt in a person's life.

Rejection by a parent as a child or rejection by a spouse, both cause a bigger void in that person's life. The question then becomes how to fill the void. There are some children who choose the wrong path in life looking for someone to fill that void caused by rejection by a parent. Rejection by a spouse also causes pain. It is bad enough when a person is abused in many ways, but she still feels that somehow she is loved by that person. The problem becomes compounded when she is abused and then finds out that she is really not loved or that there is someone else who shares her spouse's affection. What does a victim do when she is already "beat down" by years of abuse? Some victims allow the infidelity to continue without saying anything. They pretend that it doesn't exist or some join in the inappropriate sexual behaviors, voluntarily or involuntarily, which is more abuse. Some victims try to put a stop to the infidelity while staying in the marriage, enduring more abuse. Then, other victims finally get the courage to fight back. That void caused by rejection can continue to cycle just like the abuse can cycle by the decisions that are made. Some people fight infidelity with infidelity to get back at the spouse. That only causes more wounds with shame, regret, etc. The choice to be courageous and fight back to not take it any longer is the hardest choice, but it is the one that leads to the most healing.

For some, infidelity is the final line that is crossed. Some victims may have taken the abuse for years but believed that their spouses were faithful to them. The unfaithfulness of a spouse is the "last straw", and they become motivated to demand change. This is not an easy decision and a very difficult battle to initiate especially when the victim is already dealing with a manipulative, deceptive, lying person to begin with. To be courageous and set limits on behavior is like drawing a line in the sand. Will the line be crossed and what will be the consequences? Do you save the marriage

or end it? The victim finally has to be strong enough to stand by her decision—stay or leave…

This is where my story continues again…

Years of abuse, but I always thought my husband was faithful. Years
of being falsely accused of looking at other men, but I was never thinking that my husband had looked at other women. Years of being called
fat only followed by "just joking." Years of being called stupid, ignorant,
crazy, etc—was always followed by "just joking". Years of being called lazy
even while he sat at home for years while I worked and supported him.
New vehicles purchased almost every few years, as well as new boats, new
campers—just to keep peace in the house. I gave in to almost anything just
to make my husband happy. A new vehicle was bought three months after
buying another new one—just because he didn't like the color. He claimed
to get all his money back on the trade-in, and I ignorantly believed him.
He also would lie and blame me for always wanting something new which
I found out later when my own parents asked me why I always wanted
him to buy new vehicles. Vehicle after vehicle, toy after toy, trip after trip
were all bought or done to just please my husband. And I was so naïve that
I didn't question his motive. I always knew that I was truthful, so I never
suspected that he wasn't. What I didn't realize at the time was the truth of
that scripture, **"Out of the abundance of the heart, the mouth speaks."**
Almost everything that he accused me, were things he actually had done.

The day that I found out that he was unfaithful to me was absolutely
devastating. I had suffered through years of emotional and verbal abuse but
always believed that he still loved me. The episodes of violence always kept
me on edge, as I was just waiting for another to occur. I had always given
in to his demands. To hear that he had not loved me for 16 years, since
before our first child was born was totally devastating. Then, **he told me**

that he never really loved me. He also informed me that he had planned to divorce me before I had gotten pregnant with our first child—**that was why he was so angry.** I felt that my heart had been ripped out of my chest. We had three children! How could this happen! How could someone be so deceptive? I was totally crushed. I felt totally used. This man had repeatedly told me how much he loved me and was now telling me that he lied. In fact, he told me that he waited until he was prepared to leave. He told me that he purposefully held me and "made love" to me to trick me and use me; he actually said that he used me just for sex. We had gone to a marriage counselor previously because he had gotten so mean to me, and I had told him a year prior to leave. We were doing what the counselor had advised and were going on dates every other week to spend time together. He had told me and the counselor that we did not need to go anymore because our marriage was great. I had told the counselor then that I felt that he was having an affair with a woman, but my husband had adamantly denied it. He had manipulated and lied to me, and the counselor could not see through his lies. My husband was the type of person that could look another in the eyes and lie to his face without any sign of nervousness or remorse. Amazingly, I had always said that he could probably pass a lie detector test without any problem, and I was probably correct in that assumption. He had pretended to be a loving husband. He had pretended to desire me but had only used me to get what he wanted. I had just been that "toy or rag doll" that he played with when he wanted and then put back on the shelf when he was through. It was just like I had felt when we were first married years before.

He had brought a couple and their three children into our home as family friends while the woman and he were having an affair. He had met her at work. How blind could I have been!! This woman and I had sat in my vehicle three weeks before this time, professing our love for our husbands and saying that we would never leave them. This woman had asked me why I allowed my husband to verbally and emotionally abuse me the way that he did. She recognized the abuse and commented about how bad he treated me!! I told her that I loved him and hoped that he would change one day. Now, they wanted to be together. I was so blind! I was so naïve! He had convinced me that we were all just friends.

We spent so much money always buying him new things and doing things to make him happy. He has used me and manipulated me for years. So many thoughts came flooding into my mind. My mind was whirling. He told me that he really did love me, but he was "in love" with her. The marriage counselor told him that "Love was what was left over when the "in love" is gone. I was so hurt, so confused, and so broken. I could not think straight. I was told at that time that he wanted to try to save our marriage, and that the other people were trying to save their marriage. I agreed to try, but **I drew the line in the sand—NO MORE TALKING TO THAT WOMAN.** Well, that only lasted a few days before I heard his cell phone ring late one night; it was her. I told him to leave as he was walking out the door. Our oldest son, who was fifteen years old at the time, helped me as we packed his bags that night for me to kick him out of the house the next day. My son kept telling me that I did not deserve to be treated the way that his dad treated me and told me to kick him out. Even though I had tried to protect my children, they actually had seen more than I did. I had been totally blind to what had been going on under my own nose.

Through all of this turmoil, I remembered what had been told to me years before and the realization of what it meant finally struck me! This man that I had fallen in love with and innocently married had manipulated me for years. He told me a few months after we were married that his best friend—the one that my sister and I played croquet with—had actually told him years before we even met that I "was the nicest person anyone could ever meet!" **He also told him that he "wasn't good enough for someone like me" and then even told that "<u>I was too good for him to ever even date!</u>"**

His comment to me a few months after we were married was, **"<u>But I showed them!</u>"………"<u>I married you!</u>"**…

Oh my God! My whole married life was a lie too!! He never really loved me! I had been the victim of what became a challenge to him. He had always told me to never tell him that he could not do something because he would prove me wrong. He would do it just to show me that he could. He had been told that I was too good for him. He had been told that he wasn't good enough for me and that he could never date someone like me. These words had become a challenge to him when he was teenager. He had watched me for years from a distance. He knew all about me before we met. The realization hit me like a lightening bolt after all of those years. The shock was massive. I had been the one thing that he was told that he could never have. The pain in my heart and soul was totally indescribable. I had been an innocent victim in his game of challenge. I was totally crushed—completely pulverized!

CHAPTER 9

The Whirlwind Begins

"Even if my father and mother abandon me,
the Lord will hold me close."
Psalm 27:10(NLT)

When a marriage falls apart, someone gets hurt. The person that gets hurt is usually the innocent one, the one who didn't even realize that something was deteriorating in the relationship. The person who wants out of the relationship is already ready to move on in most cases, so the deep pain is not evident in that person. In an abusive relationship, the abuser typically is very deceptive with his actions. He uses control, manipulation, intimidation, and deception to get what he wants. This is not any different when he is unfaithful to his spouse. When a victim of an abusive spouse loses that spouse, he/she is still hurt. When an abused spouse becomes the victim of infidelity, that hurt is compounded again. These are more wounds inflicted on an already wounded person. Though life was not perfect, that was the life that he/she knew and that life is totally changed. The family unit is changed. The innocent victim becomes the victim again. Everything that was familiar to that person is altered in some way.

The emotions that people go through during those initial hours, days, and weeks are like a whirlwind, especially if they were blindsided. The devastation is indescribable. Sometimes the description should be pulverized. Many people, men and women, become victims of infidelity and feel this total destruction. Everything that they believed as a person or believed in a person seems wrong. The person that they trusted the most as a spouse has lied to them. The person that they shared their lives with and their deepest heart-felt feelings has lied to them. All these thoughts keep flying around their heads like a hurricane, going around and around. When? Where? How? The destruction of a hurricane can be massive, just like the breakup of a marriage. It affects everyone—parent, child, family, friend, property, etc. What was real? What was truth? What were lies? So many questions! But, are the answers they get truthful? Where is the trust? Trust is one of the basic foundations of a marriage. When trust is destroyed, what do you have left? What do you do? The key is to take it one tiny step at a time and pray.

The first tiny step most people take is to just cry, pouring out your heart. The crying may even be heart wrenching, deep sobbing cries from deep within the soul. It is a cry that can't be imitated; it can't be mocked. Those sobs come from so deep within your body that it is not even identifiable as a cry. It is a cry from years of wounds. It is like every wound that has ever been experienced has opened up and cries out for healing. It is like the body has been turned inside out. It feels like one is exploding. Some may feel like they are imploding. They may feel like their hearts are bursting. The pain feels unbearable. How can they go on? Everything that they have ever known to be true is now lies. How can someone be so deceptive? Some are so hurt that they literally feel like they are dying inside, or they may wish that they could die to ease the pain.

This is where my story continues again…

I was this victim—again. I totally trusted. I was totally blindsided. I was probably ignorant to be so trusting, but I would never think of having an affair, so I did not suspect anything. I believed his lies. The one time that I questioned his behavior with other women was met with a violent outburst. Yelling, screaming, and cursing at me was followed by him throwing a box at me. As his present hit me in the chest, he yelled for me to give it to someone that I trusted since I didn't trust him. His violence always scared me and our children. He demanded that I trust him. He insisted that he was not doing anything and that we were all just friends. This woman, her husband, and their three children spent many hours in our home as family friends. I believed him because I thought we were all family friends. It had been so long since we had friends that would visit us as a family. We went boat riding together, played cards together, and cooked together. I never looked at her husband, so why would my husband look at her. I truly felt that marriage is forever. It was not logical to me to even look at another person. When you give your heart to someone, it is forever. He had my heart and had just crushed it. I believed that marriage is a covenant vow taken before God, for better or worse. I had experienced years of worse and had always hoped for the better to come.

The day after that late night phone call, we officially separated. I had drawn the line in the sand, and he crossed it when he spoke to her again. I somehow got the strength to tell him that I did not deserve to be second best. He had already planned to marry her. She left her husband again. So many memories were whirling around in my head. Years of pain and suffering, years of fear, years of heartache were all mixed with hopes for a brighter future. The tears were unstoppable. The sobs were heart wrenching. For hours and days, I experienced that indescribable wailing from deep within my soul. I screamed out for the Lord to help me. Calls were put out for all my family and friends. The cavalry came to gather around me for support, but no words of encouragement helped. My family, whom I had left many years before to be with him, all surrounded me to help in my time of need. Some had seen the control. Some had seen the abuse. Several had warned me about marrying him in the first place many years before. No comfort would come to me for a long time. Everyone saw what was happening but me. Even my children had noticed the looks between my husband and the other woman during the entire summer. My children had suffered in silence, not knowing how to tell me that something was wrong and how their dad had been behaving while I worked. My heart was broken. I could not get enough strength to comfort my own children. I was devastated. I felt that I had been hanging on by a thread for many years, and that thread had just snapped. It was like I was falling, falling, falling.

So many thoughts of the past flew like a whirlwind in my head. He had gotten angry a few years after we were married around the time his dad died, and he quit work to go to school. I had supported him during those two years, always thinking that he would support me one day. We had three children, and I had planned to switch to part-time work and be home more when we were financially stable. He had gotten angry when our youngest child was a newborn and voluntarily quit a well-paying job. After several months of drinking and job rejections, he took a straight night shift job making minimum wage as a police officer. His five dollars an hour salary barely paid the day care for the three children. He had the ideal big boy job, playing cops and robbers. He was so excited to go to work on his scheduled shift, and he worked for no pay on nights when he should have been home with his family. The baby did not even know him. She cried when he tried to hold her or feed her. When a straight day-shift job came open, I begged him to take it. However, it was on a police motor-cycle. Well, I got the blame for that when he got in a terrible wreck with a bus and had severe injuries.

I took him home in a hospital bed with multiple injuries and uncontrollable pain. I tried to take care of him and work. Physical therapists came to the house to help him walk again. His family helped a lot, but he got angrier and angrier. He would constantly yell at me and our children. Our oldest was only nine years old, and he was taking on the responsibility to help with the yard like an adult. I worked during the day, bathed him and took care of him and the children at night, then stayed up till 1:00 or 2:00 in the mornings doing laundry and cleaning house after everyone was asleep. Amazingly, I was later accused of doing absolutely nothing and that he had to do everything. I was physically and emotionally drained, but I knew that I had to keep my family going. The only people who saw my exhaustion were my co-workers who worked with me during the day. Our children were only 3, 6, and 9 years old at the time of the wreck. I kept praying for healing for him, strength to keep going, and a brighter future for all of us.

I worked and supported my husband during the next five years as he went back to school to get a teaching certificate. He had been told that he could not return to police work due to his physical limitations. He was very angry with me and the entire world, and he took it out on me and the children. He decided that he wanted to be a special education teacher. I tried to tell him that he did not have patience with our own children, so how could he have patience with other children, especially special needs children. He insisted on being a special education teacher. It was during his very first teaching job that he met the other woman. After five years of supporting him while he went to school again, I would not even see a year's salary before our breakup. All of my hopes for a brighter future for my family were smashed in that instance.

Many memories whirled around my head. Many hurtful words were spoken to me in those few days. He told me that he <u>never</u> really loved me!

59

He also told me that he hadn't loved me for at least sixteen years, since before our first child was born. He told me that he only stayed with me for the children. Many times he told me that he could kill me and would know how to hide my body where no one would ever find it. He repeatedly said that he could make it look like an accident or that I had just left. He said that no one would ever know the truth. He had an arsenal of guns in his possession. He repeatedly threatened to accidentally shoot me while cleaning his guns. He even reminded me that he was a police officer and could get away with it. His friends would believe him. He would go partying with his police friends, coming home drunk, and get up just a few hours later and go to work. They all protected each other. He repeatedly threatened to hit me. I frequently watched him throw things or hit the walls. He had put his fist through our son's bedroom door in anger when he was mad at him one day. The anger that he had bottled up in him exploded into violence at times. Now, the anger was being poured out in very hurtful words. He told me that he lied as he held me and told me that he loved me daily until he was ready to leave. He told me that he manipulated me over the last year while he planned all of this. He told me that he couldn't stand me, and that I was fat and ugly. He repeatedly told me that I was mean and hateful. He told me that I was selfish and controlling. He said that no one liked me and people even hated being around me. I remembered periods of his drunkenness when he tried to wreck the vehicle as I drove home with our three children in the backseat. The kids and I were screaming for him to stop grabbing the steering wheel and yanking it around. There had been several kegs of beer, and he knew no limit when there was free alcohol. I remembered him wrecking at another friend's house years before because he was so drunk and missed the driveway. There was so much cursing, yelling, and screaming over all the years, but I still loved him. I never lied to him about how I felt about him. I never manipulated him. I tried to be a loving, caring wife, but that was all gone now. I couldn't think. All that I could do was cry as all of these memories flooded my mind. But I had to go on. I had three children that needed their mom. I had to think about their future and continue to pray.

I kept begging God to forgive me. I prayed for God to forgive me for any disobedience and any way that I had failed Him. I felt that maybe I was being punished for something that I did or maybe didn't do. I did not believe in divorce. I did not want my children growing up in a "broken" home. Growing up as a Catholic, I truly believed that if I divorced him, I would be condemned to spend eternity in hell. Divorce was a dreadful word in my mind that brought much condemnation. I did not know the Word of God and did not realize that God does not want his children abused, and that God allowed divorce when a spouse committed adultery. All of these thoughts played havoc with my emotions. I was hurt beyond description. However, I could not see and could not realize that God was always in control and protected the innocent.

I tell you that any person that divorces his wife (or her husband) and marries another woman (or man) is guilty of the sin of adultery. The only reason for a person to divorce and marry again is if his first wife (or her husband) had sexual relations with another..." Matthew 19:9 (NKJV)

CHAPTER 10

The Breakup

"I can do all things through Christ who strengthens me."
Philippians 4:13(NKJV)

The next step when the uncontrolled crying decreases, is to think about the plans for the immediate future. All the wounds of the past may keep whirling around as memories, but somehow, you need to put one foot in front of the other and keep walking. It is very hard to discuss a breakup with someone that you love, but the children have to come first. The children have two parents, and they cannot be used as a pawn in a game between parents. Who will the children live with? Who will get what? Is it a trial separation or the final breakup? So many questions need to be answered in the midst of so much pain. The person who is doing the walking out has probably already planned everything out since they are usually prepared. The children may have something to say about whom they want to live with, but the legal system will make the final decision regarding the children. Then the question is still, will it get that far? Is this marriage salvageable or not? Most people would think that a victim of abuse would be shouting for joy that his/her abuser is gone. However, it is not that easy. That person, even though he abused his spouse, was still a significant person in the victim's life. The breakup of a marriage with all the things that are said and done is so destructive; it becomes another wound in the life of "the walking wounded."

Again, my story continues…

Many hurtful thoughts were whirling in my head like a hurricane. The pain in my head from crying and the "weight of the world" on my shoulders seemed unbearable. I felt that my whole life had been a lie. However, I had children to put first—they were not a lie. I truly believed that they were a gift from the Lord. Unfortunately, my husband was still controlling me. How did I break that control after so many years?

He said that this separation was only a trial and that he still wanted to be friends. He was staying with his sister only a few doors away. His family members were in and out, daily proclaiming their love for me. They all kept saying that I would always be family. It was especially rough the day after the separation since it was my birthday. What a birthday present that was! I did not realize the significance of this "birthday present" until many years later when I realized that I was healed. My "birthday" had actually been the first day or the birth of freedom from that man and his abuse. However, I could not see it at the time. Many tears continued to flow, but the initial plan was set. We would share the kids, alternating weekends during this trial separation. The big thing was that he demanded that <u>we would stay friends</u>!

He would frequently call every day just to talk. He would stop by to drink coffee and visit. He would stop by the house to see us morning and night. He would hug us and kiss us. I could not tell him "no." He still had that control over me. He was constantly changing his mind and saying different things. He kept saying that the other woman's children were all hurt because they missed him and our children. I kept telling him that our own children were hurt and did not want to have anything to do with those people. The children were all very angry with him, but he did not want to believe it. He was blind to anything that could be considered as being wrong on his part. The children had joyfully gone through the entire house the day that we split up and dumped bottle after bottle of bourbon, whiskey, rum, vodka, wine, etc into the sink. Any alcoholic beverage was thrown out. All three of the children repeatedly said that they could not stand how he acted, especially when he was drinking. They were actually somewhat relieved that he was out of the house. But none of them could tell him that.

There was one day right after we separated that he showed up at my house and wanted me to go ride with him to a piece of land that we owned. We had actually had the house pad built early that summer to build a house, but he had stopped the contractor from starting the house the day before he was scheduled to begin construction. I later realized that he was already planning to leave. The wood, the cables, and supplies had been delivered and were on the land, ready to begin. However, he had cancelled everything. He said that we needed to go to discuss the land. He was being very nice at that moment, so I went with him. Once we got there, he started trying to go through the ditch with his topless jeep. This ditch was huge, like the size of a big truck. I kept pleading with him to stop and to not go through the ditch because we would roll over. He started yelling that I did not have faith in him. He was yelling that I did not trust him and "How can you have a marriage if you don't have trust!" I started crying and begging him to stop. We were so close to turning over, and I was holding on tight. He was terrifying me. He was acting like a crazy person. I kept praying for God to help me. Also, in his anger, he went to the small area of woods on the edge of the property and started ramming the jeep into the trees. He kept yelling at me that I did not trust him. He would ram the front of the jeep into a tree, and then put it in reverse and ram the back of the jeep into a tree. He ended up getting us wedged between two trees with damage to the front and back of the vehicle. He managed to get us out while bragging about his driving capabilities. He had gone from nice and sweet to mean and dangerous in minutes. I was trembling and crying. How can you stay friends with someone like that? But he kept threatening to fight for the children if I didn't stay friends with him.

He told me that he was enjoying his life. It was like he had the best of both worlds—his girlfriend on one side and his wife and kids on the other. He spoke to whom he wanted and when. He saw whom he wanted and when. No boundaries. No one to answer to! He was married but a free man. He was totally happy with the situation. I was still devastated and miserable. The healing could not even begin when multiple calls a day were received from him. He always wanted to know what I was doing, but I was too weak emotionally to tell him that it was no longer his business. His family would invite me over to visit, and we would all sit together and talk, until his phone would ring and then he would leave to talk in private to his other woman. I just kept talking to him like an obedient wife. His brother and sister had all had affairs and their spouses stayed friends with them, even staying together in marriage. They all expected us to just stay friends like it was no big deal, one big happy family. The children would go spend the night with him and come back reporting that he stayed on the phone with his girlfriend and did not even talk to them. They repeatedly said that he ignored them and would yell at them if they interrupted him. They were absolutely miserable also. This was not how a normal family should behave.

The children had seen a lot over the previous months. My oldest did not want to have anything to do with his dad. He had not liked the way his dad had behaved for years. My children kept saying that they did not like the other woman's children who had been brought into our house. My middle child reported getting beaten while I was at work because one of her children had reported lies to him. My youngest reported that her dad never read bedtime stories to her until the other child came to spend the night. He had been trying to win over the other children while forsaking our own children. I realized that our children were smarter than we had given them credit for, and they were more observant to what was going on around them. But I knew that they were still hurting. He was still their dad.

Within a short period of time, I made an appointment with a counselor for the children and me to talk to. I was too emotional to trust myself to make the right decisions regarding my children so I sought the advice of professionals. That was probably the wisest decision that I made at the time. The counselor became an advocate for my children. She identified the abuse immediately, whereas the marriage counselor had been totally manipulated by my husband. I didn't even realize how much my children would need an advocate in the future because I couldn't see past the present pain that I was living in. The children could be honest about their feelings with the counselor. They could tell her how they really felt and how they really feared their dad.

The children were having trouble sleeping. My youngest son was acting out in anger and fighting more with his siblings. He cried one day and said, "Why didn't he tell us earlier in the summer that he loved someone else instead of waiting till the week before school starts!" They were having trouble in school. They could not concentrate. One day, their dad came by to help with their homework but started yelling at them. He had no patience with children; yet he had insisted on becoming a special education teacher. The children were actually getting more upset when their dad was with them than when they were apart. They saw how their dad lashed out at all of us. They told me that they could tell a difference in the house being more peaceful with him gone. However, they were still upset and had to have someone to talk to about their feelings. Their dad was always yelling at them because they did not want to go visit him. The counselor listened and became a friend to them—someone that they could confide in. There was no scheming or no manipulations on my part. I could not foretell the future. I was just trying to make it hour by hour to get through the haze that I existed in at that moment in my life.

CHAPTER 11

The Impossible Task

"God blesses those who mourn, for they will be comforted."
Matthew 5:4(NLT)

Manipulators and deceivers are similar to spiders, weaving all of these intricate webs that people can get caught in. The manipulative and deceptive abuser controls the spouse for so long that the victim can no longer stand up for herself. She is caught in this trap. In most cases, she can't see the truth any longer. All that the victim knows is what has been spoon fed to her. Others may see the truth from outside of that situation but the victim, after years of being emotionally, verbally, and/ or physically abused, is many times blind to the truth. When an abusive spouse wants a separation or divorce from his spouse, but wants to stay friends just like nothing ever happened, it is just to be able to continue to control that person and the situation. It is like the old saying, "having your cake and eating it too." Who is benefitted by this friendship situation? It is definitely not the victim. The victim has been unable to stand up for herself when they were together and continues to be controlled and manipulated as long as she "talks" to him as a friend.

The best thing is for the victim to set boundaries and stick to them. Also, seeking professional counseling for her and the children will give someone on the outside the information that is being fed to them to help decipher truth versus lies. A counselor in this situation can help to guide the victim through the darkness. After years of abuse, it is very hard for an emotionally abused person to be independent overnight. Sometimes, the victim needs help to get emotionally stronger to fight back and become independent from their controlling spouse. Any resistance from the victim can result in more violence from the abuser. The abuser does not want to lose that control over his victim, and that anger and violence has always been the ultimate control that brought the victim back under his power. Consequently, it is very important for the victim to have family, friends, clergy, coworkers, and counselors available to help her during this trying time where a potential of abuse is elevating as they try to get control back in their own lives.

This is where my story continues again…

He made the decision to separate, to have a girlfriend, to remain friends with me, to see the kids when he wanted, to talk to me several times a day as he desired, and to even hold and kiss me when he wanted. I just could not put up any resistance to anything. I was still very emotional, and I was holding on to the hope that we could reconcile. I was even invited to family get-togethers with him and his family. They continued to tell me that I would always be part of the family, no matter what happened. Well, within a week of our arrangement, during a family cook-out, he calmly told me while he was drinking that he had made a decision. He told me that he wanted 4 things—money, land, a divorce, and her! He told me to find an attorney for a non-contested divorce. He said that $500 would get us an attorney without a fight. He also said that if I fought him on anything he wanted or did not maintain a friendship with him, that he would fight me for half of everything plus custody of the kids. He also asked me about the kids being upset with him. I mistakenly invited him over to the house for him to talk to the kids that night. I thought that he would believe the children instead of hearing how they actually felt from me.

Later that night after much drinking, he showed up at "our" house very drunk to talk to me and the three children. He told the kids that we were going to get a divorce and asked them how they felt about everything. I ignorantly encouraged them to tell their dad the truth. As the children started telling him about how upset they really were that he brought this woman and her kids into our home, that he had broken up our family, and that they were angry with him for the way that he had been treating all of us, he exploded into a violent outburst. He was yelling and screaming with his fists clenched. He continuously screamed, cursing and telling the kids how ungrateful they were for all he had done for them. He went on a rampage, yelling that he had been the mother, the father—that he had done everything for them. (He had stayed home for 5 years after his wreck while I had worked.) He was yelling that he was the one getting up with them when they were sick at night. (I remember not being able to wake him up since they were all babies when they were sick and crying.) He yelled at them and threatened them that he was coming back in the morning. He screamed at them that they better each have one good thing to tell him about what he had done for them or else. He stormed out of the house, peeling out in the yard with tires squealing. The kids and I all huddled together, crying. I was so sorry for putting them in that situation, not realizing that he would become violent again. I had failed to protect my children and had even invited him into the house, never anticipating another violent outburst—especially when he was asking them to be honest and tell him the truth! How can someone ask children to tell them the truth—how they really feel—then blast them and threaten them? It did not make any sense, especially since what he had said was not true. His view of what had really happened was so distorted. He either believed his own lies or something was really wrong with him. (I later had to ask my own children the truth as to who did what for them thinking that maybe I was the crazy one. They had all told me that they did not ask their dad to do anything for them because he was always so angry and fussing. They would wait for me to get home from work to help them with whatever they needed.)

As we all listened to him tearing down the road with tires squealing in anger to his sister's house, we were all terrified and trembling. The children cried and asked what they were going to tell him in the morning. They were afraid that he was going to beat them if he was not happy with their answers. I told them that all they had to say was that they loved him. Then, the phone rang! He was so angry! He told me to get ready! He yelled that he was coming in the morning and taking half of everything and was fighting me for custody of the children. He accused me of turning his kids against him. Then, he hung up in a fit of rage.

I was trembling and crying. The kids were crying hysterically. We were all so afraid of his violent outbursts. What could I do? How could I protect us? It was at that moment that I decided to call on family and friends again. My parents had decided to stay in their camper nearby in case I needed them, and a neighbor had offered to help if I needed him. It was near midnight, but I called for help. Within a short period of time, my dad and neighbor had all of my locks changed on my house with new keys. My husband, who wanted his girlfriend, a divorce, money, land, and to be friends with me had just lost access to the house that we had shared together as a family. I had to protect me and my children! It was the first time that I had taken a stand against him.

The phone rang again at 7am with more yelling and screaming. The children and I were still sleeping because we had been up most of the night. The two youngest had fallen asleep in my room. He had come to open the door with his key and all of the locks had been changed. He was hysterical! I kept praying and pleading with the Lord to help us. He was acting crazy again! How dare I change the locks and lock him out of his own house! I told him that he was scaring the kids by his behavior. I reminded him that he asked them to tell him the truth about how they felt then he went off on them in a rampage when they were trying to tell him the truth. I told him that we were afraid of him, and that he needed to stop acting like that. He did not want to hear the truth! He blamed me for everything. He threatened again to get custody of the children from me as well as the house and his half of everything that we owned.

He screamed to me that now I had done it! Now I had really made him mad! How dare I lock him out of his own house!! He was going to fight me now! He wanted half of everything plus the kids! He repeatedly accused me of turning his kids against him. He screamed at me that I was crazy. He could not see what he was doing to his own children. He was totally blind to his own abusive behavior. He always felt that he was right, never wrong. The last thing that he screamed at me before he slammed down the phone was,

"You are going to pay for what you have done to me!"

CHAPTER 12

The Rollercoaster

"Unless the Lord builds a house, the work of the builders is useless."
Psalm 127:1 (NLT)

During the time of a marital breakup, there are so many emotions flowing on both sides—anger, resentment, hurt, fear, confusion, etc. The fluctuations that are seen in an abusive person's personality are even more wide spread—especially if it is that person that wants out of the marriage. An abusive person has always been in control in the relationship. He probably felt deep down that his spouse and girl friend would accept the current situation as well and remain in both relationships. However, for some reason, the choice is made and the decision is made to move forward in one direction or another. When the decision is to save a marriage, then both parties have to be totally willing to work together, to forgive, and possibly work with a counselor to save what is left of the marriage. When the decision is made to end the marriage, it can either be peaceful or a battle. The legal system allows non-contested divorces where both parties agree on custody of children and division of assets. It is very important to get an attorney to represent the victim who probably can't think through the turmoil in her life. The dissolution of a marriage is very painful, especially to the innocent spouse. However, many times the spouse wanting the divorce also has many mixed feelings and the pendulum can swing from one emotion to another very quickly. It is like being on an emotional rollercoaster with emotional highs and lows going from anger and violence to sorrow and remorse. These uncertainties only cause more confusion and wounds to the innocent person. When so many things are said back and forth, how can a person tell what is the truth? The One who knows all truth is the Lord. He sees all. He knows all. The key is to turn to Him. One thing that is true is that a marriage made with God in it is not easily broken. The Lord is the foundation, the Rock, which all things should be built upon. Those who turn to Him during these difficult times will eventually see that He did guide their path and protect them.

"Trust in the Lord with all your heart; Do not depend on your own understanding. Seek his will in all you do, and he will direct your paths." Proverbs 3:5-6(NLT)

Here is where my story continues again…

The day after I locked my husband out of the house after his violent outburst with the children, was another rollercoaster of emotion day. He called yelling, screaming, cursing, and threatening me at 7:00 am and then hung up on me. Later that day, he called very remorseful for his behavior and wanted to come over to talk. Again, I agreed, but we met on the carport and agreed to discuss the children and division of assets. I would not let him in the house near the children. The children had cried most of the night after his emotional, verbal, and threatening attack on them. They were terrified of him!

He had changed his mind again. He was going back and forth in what he really wanted to do. He then told me that he had already made a list of what he wanted, and I then made a list of what I wanted. We both signed them to give to an attorney. He calmly told me then that he wanted me to get an attorney to file for divorce—a non-contested divorce. I told him that I wanted to file based on adultery which would give us an immediate divorce. He refused to allow me to file with adultery and stated that if I tried that, he would fight me for half of everything and custody of the kids. He kept accusing me of turning the kids against him. I boldly told him that day that his relationship with his children was his responsibility—his behavior would either make it or break it. He never saw that and continued to accuse me of turning his kids against him.

The next day, I called an attorney that was recommended by friends. I was told that the next available appointment was over a month from then. I begged the receptionist to find a slot and offered to pay double to meet with him that day. I hung up the phone while praying for God to help me. I called back a few hours later and was told that I did not have to pay double; an appointment had been cancelled. That attorney was now available to meet with me that afternoon. I got all of the information that I could together, with the lists created and signed the day before, and met with this attorney. I told him the entire story and told him that I wanted a divorce that day. He laughingly told me that it didn't work that quick and that it could take months. I insistently told him that I could not wait that long. I needed it done right then because I knew my husband; he would change his mind and play with my emotions. The attorney called his paralegal into his office, told her to drop everything else, and asked her to work on my case. They would make it a priority and take care of it as soon as possible.

Within hours of filing for divorce with my new attorney, I received a phone call from my husband. He was doing just what I had anticipated. He was crying—for the first time. He was feeling sick. He said that he did not want to lose me. He did not want the divorce after all of this. He told me that he really loved me. He said that he had just been confused. I told him that it was too late—the process was already in motion. He begged me to cancel. I reminded him that he was the one who told me to file, and he was the one who said that he wanted a new life and a new wife. He was remorseful for the first time. At that time I finally got enough strength to tell him that I would not stop the divorce. If he truly loved me, he could date me and prove it to me after the divorce was finalized. He was not happy with that answer either. I was convinced that he really did not know what he wanted. However, I knew that he could not really love me. The things that he had told me would not come out of the mouth of someone who truly loved me. Again, he actually called me later that day and said that he really did <u>not</u> love me and wanted the divorce after all. His *"love me"* versus *"love me not"* words flowed like a faucet being turned on and off several times a day. His behavior was absolutely crazy, but I couldn't see it because I had lived in that abusive situation for years with him blowing up in anger over something and then changing his mind within hours. He had intimidated me and harassed me for years. Consequently, even though we were separated, he still had that control over me.

Less than three weeks from the day that we separated, all of the legal papers with a petition for divorce, the child custody, and the property settlement were signed by the judge. The attorney had said that it could take months, but papers were pushed through quickly. We just had to wait six months or so for the final divorce. A couple of weeks after the judge signed those legal documents, I had to attend a court-ordered parenting class. Every other person in that class was joking and laughing, having a good time. I was still very emotional and crying the entire time. I could not stop crying as I thought about my children and my marriage falling apart. Everyone in that class had been separated for months or years. It had been about a month since my whole life had gotten turned upside down. Everything was happening so fast. It was unheard of for a petition for divorce with the child custody and property settlement to be done so quickly. I just knew that the emotional rollercoaster would not stop so this petition for divorce had to be done immediately. My husband always played with my emotions and I could not decipher truth from lies at that time or anytime. He had always controlled me with his manipulations, lies, and deceit. Unfortunately, I still hung on to everything that he told me as truth.

The counselor was so concerned about me during this parenting class that she spoke to me after the class. She became my counselor from that time forward. She quickly identified the abuse that I had lived under and became an advocate for me. The children had their counselor who also identified the abuse we had been under and was an advocate for the children. I did not realize at that time how important those advocates would become in the future. I also did not realize until much later how God had His Hand over me and guided me through this most difficult time and even orchestrated the entire legal situation for me. I was walking through a fog going to work and taking care of the children, as well as talking to my husband and his family daily. The emotional rollercoaster with my husband would not stop, but God was guiding my path.

CHAPTER 13

The Turmoil

*"The steps of the godly are directed by the Lord. He delights in every detail
of their lives. Though they stumble, they will not fall,
for the Lord holds them by the hand."*
Psalm37:23-24(NLT)

Remaining friends with an abusive spouse is probably not the best thing to do, especially in the process of a divorce. The harassment, intimidation, and other abusive ways don't change, and it only benefits the abuser. The emotional and verbal abuse just hits new levels. The manipulations don't change. An abusive person manages with "half-truths", not total lies, but not total truth as well. Words become manipulated to suit the person or situation. They are clever enough to say what each person would want to hear. Protecting children in that situation is very difficult. How do you protect children when they are in a joint custody situation? How do you protect children from witnessing adultery and thinking that it is acceptable? How do you protect children when they have already tried to tell their true feelings and were threatened? Unfortunately, the courts don't recognize verbal and emotional abuse until a life is threatened or physical injury occurs. The best thing to do is to have an advocate, a counselor for the children, who the children can tell what they experience with mom and with dad. The parent should not verbally bash the other parent in front of the children. The children love both parents, and they should not be used as a pawn against the other parent. Both parents should protect the children. Also, the feelings of the children should also be considered. The children have to have someone that they can speak to truthfully without having to worry about hurting a parent's feelings or being threatened. Always work with the counselor regarding information to be shared with the other parent. The children have to come first, not the friendship with the future ex…no matter what the threat is.

This is where my story continues again…

The emotional rollercoaster that I was on would not stop. I kept hearing "stay friends or I will fight for custody," "stop the divorce," "I love you," "I will always love you," "I hate you," "I love her," "I want her," etc. The words kept changing everyday. I started going to a spirit-filled church and seeking the Lord daily. I knew that the Lord knew the truth, and I could not handle all of this alone. My family had all gone home. I felt all alone except for him and his family who lived just two doors down. I had friends who were coming forward and telling me about the abuse that they had witnessed that I had been blind to for all of those years—abuse to me and my children. My coworkers had identified the abuse and tried to help me through this difficult time.

My children were very upset with their dad. All of them were having trouble sleeping. My youngest son told me as he cried one day, "I thought that I was a good son! Dad did not only walk out on you; he walked out of all of us!" He was angry and hurt. My two youngest children would sleep in my room because they were afraid. My youngest son had made a camp in his dad's now empty closet. There were nights that I could hear him crying in his "camp." Their dad would still show up several times at our house and start yelling and screaming for any little thing. He kept insisting that we stay friends or else. The children were having trouble in school, and their dad would yell at them that they better not blame him. They saw their dad at a store one day, and my son told me that his dad "shot the bird" at him in the store. They were embarrassed and upset by his behavior. All of the children told me that they did not even want him back in the house.

The children saw their dad act like a teenager with his girlfriend. They witnessed their dad kissing her, passionately, in the front yard of his sister's house. The kids were in the yard watching. She spent the entire weekend with him at his sister's house a month and a half after our separation. The kids reported that he made them hug and kiss her and tell her that they loved her. Their cousin told them that a double wide mobile home had been ordered for their dad and his new future wife and all six of the children—his and hers. My children came home so upset from their aunt's house. I made the mistake of trying to tell him at some point some of the things that made the kids upset; this was followed by yelling, cursing, and threats again. The children got upset with me because they did not want me to tell him anything about them. However, the child custody papers stated that I had to keep him informed. I made that mistake several times and then finally started asking their counselor for advice. The children did not want their dad to go to any of their counseling sessions. They did not want him to know how they really felt. They were fearful of his explosive anger.

The week after their romantic weekend at his sister's house, the woman went back to her husband...again. He actually told me that he realized how much he really loved me and wanted me back. He told me that he broke up with her to reconcile with me. As I was calling a mutual friend to tell her my good news, she told me to sit down. She wanted to tell me something. She had been sitting there and hearing the lies that he and his family were feeding to me, and she finally decided to speak up. She said that the truth was that he told her, "Well, my bxxxx left me! I guess I'll go back to my wife. At least I'll have my kids!" He was using lies and manipulation again! Well, needless to say, I did not stop the divorce. I kept telling him that if he truly loved me, then he could date me after the divorce was final. I should have told him to never talk to me again, but he still had a control over me. I told him that he had to prove that he loved me. He insisted on reconciliation, so I insisted on Christian Marriage Counseling. I told him that I demanded four things—put God first along with Christian marriage counseling (because this would never have happened if God was in our marriage), stop drinking (because he gets meaner when drinking), stop smoking (which he told me for years that he would stop), and stop talking to the other woman. We started going to a Christian marriage counselor while the kids and I went to our other counselors. I would not let him back in the house which was what he actually wanted. Our children did not want him back in the house.

I told my parents one night that we were going to counseling and may eventually get back together. My father told me that he would disown me, that I would not get a penny of inheritance because that was all that my husband wanted—MONEY. I was hysterical. Other couples go through difficulty but can get back together. Why couldn't we? I even told my parents that they had stayed together even after several affairs, so why couldn't I try to save my marriage? I had told my mother previously that the other woman's husband had called me and told me that he had a bullet with my husband's name on it in his pocket. He had told me that if he ever saw him, he would kill him. In my moment of hysteria with my dad, my dad told me that he knew someone that wanted my husband dead more than he did, meaning the other woman's husband. I asked him if he meant a hit man. At that point, my husband who heard the conversation believed that my father had hired a hit man and spread it all over to everyone. My father was saying that the other husband wanted him dead. I cried uncontrollably that my family would make me chose between them or my husband if we could reconcile. My sister-in-law and my husband gave me some pills, (about 5or 6) and she took my kids for the night since I was so upset. I didn't even question what the pills were. I was so naïve and trusting. Whatever was given to me made me like a limp noodle. I had absolutely no control of my body. I felt like I was paralyzed. I could not move. I could not talk. I was terrified that I had been overdosed. I could not even open my eyes. Every muscle was totally flaccid. My husband had his way with my body all night, and I could not even move a muscle to resist or make a sound. I could not speak or move, but I was screaming inside for him to stop. I felt so drugged and did not even know what they had given me! I also felt so stupid and used again!

My husband and his family started telling everyone that my father had hired a hit man. He even told his boss that my dad was trying to kill him which was not true. His family turned against me. My property started being vandalized. My friend, who happened to be my sister-in-law's best friend, and her husband believed the truth and started being my emotional support there. They had been seeing the truth and the lies for years. They saw the manipulations that occurred on a daily basis. They came to visit me and the children frequently. They started defending me against all the lies. Lies that I had had multiple affairs and casual sex with anyone who tried to help me were constantly being spread. My friend was even walking with me late one evening when my estranged husband called me on my cell phone. He was begging me to take him back and telling me that he had made a huge mistake. He told me again that he wanted to "blow his head off!" I finally told him to just go ahead, but to please leave a suicide note to tell the children why he had left his family and then killed himself. He wanted to go to my house to see the kids before he would kill himself. I told him no—he could not go to my house to tell the kids that and upset them! He got angry then started yelling again, calling me all kinds of horrible names. He even told me that before he put a gun to his head, he was going to put a gun to my head and blow my head off. He was trying to manipulate me again, but I was finally getting a little stronger to stand up to him. That emotional rollercoaster of his had gone up and down and all around in just a few moments. However, I finally had a friend who knew all the truth and was standing with me. She heard the conversation and saw the relentless calls that he would make until I answered him. She knew that I was not the crazy one. She had known me for years and watched the emotional and verbal abuse that my children and I had endured. We called the police after getting the advice of a neighbor who worked for the police department. We notified them that he had threatened suicide and then said that he would shoot me first. We felt that it was just another manipulation attempt. I had fallen for it many times over the years, begging him not to talk like that and crying many times. The police came, his friends, and recommended that I get a restraining order or protective order to protect me from him. I notified my attorney of the events the next day. Years later, I found out from my friend that he had even gone to his sister's house while our friend was visiting and told them all that I was constantly calling him and was threatening to kill myself. He was constantly telling his family lies about me. My friend, who was still my sister-in-law's best friend at that time, told her that she was with me and that she had witnessed the relentless calls that he made to me, also overhearing his suicide threat. She told them that he was lying to his own family and tried to take up for me, but they always believed his lies. In fact, my sister-in-law came to my house one day and told me that I better leave her best friend alone. She did not want us to talk anymore. She said that she was her friend, not mine. I told her that I had known her also for over twenty years. I informed our friend that I was told not to talk to her anymore. She responded that no one was going to tell her who she could be friends with. She also said that she was seeing who was truthful and who was not.

Over the next several months, he continued in this rollercoaster of emotions and brought me along for the ride. Trying to stay friends with him was hurting me even more than I realized, but he kept threatening to fight me in court for the children if I did not talk to him. He bought land, moved into the country (about 35 to 40 minutes away), and insisted on the kids going every other weekend. The kids would beg me to not make them go, but we had to follow the court order. The kids came home crying one weekend after he had left them all alone for about six hours with no phone, no television, and no air conditioner while he went to the store. They had gotten afraid when they had no way to contact me or their dad. My son felt that he had gone to secretly see his girlfriend again. They were back together secretly, but she was still with her husband. She did not want to lose custody of her three children, and her husband had told her that he would fight for custody. My friend was still best friends with my sister-in-law and would keep me updated on what the truth actually was. My children would also confide in her, so she knew all of the truth.

My children were getting more and more upset with their dad and his behavior. My oldest child and I sat on his bed one day while he broke down and cried uncontrollably. He had told me that he felt like a 30 year old man trapped in a 16 year old body. He said that all of his life, we had taught him right from wrong. He said that he had always tried to do what was right, but now he was watching his dad drink, party, and chase women.

He felt that he was more mature than his dad. My youngest son also was so upset with his dad for his behavior. On our son's thirteenth birthday, his dad would not let him see me "because it was his weekend." But he made my son call the other woman and tell her that he loved her. They no longer wanted to go visit him and did not trust him. My oldest son did not have to go see him because he was old enough to make that decision according to the courts. However, I was getting the blame from their dad for turning the children against him. I was telling the children every day to call their dad, but they did not want to. The only ones who knew the truth were our mutual friend and her husband, whom the kids would confide in, and the counselors. My friend was also the only one there who would see the multiple calls that he would make to me daily, declaring his love to me. Then she would hear him tell his sister that I was always calling and bothering him. He would hug and kiss me but only after he looked in the direction of his sister's house to see if anyone was looking. He would then tell his family that I would not leave him alone. My children kept telling me to leave him alone. They felt that he was only using me. Our youngest child would hang onto me while her dad was visiting. It was like she was trying to protect me. He would get angry and yell at her. He would yell at me to do something with her. I knew that she was just afraid. But he had no compassion regarding their feelings. One day he screamed at her, "Don't worry—I don't want your mother!" Then, he stormed out of the house. He was still telling me that he loved me and wanted me back. I was still telling him that he needed to comply with my requests for him to change. He was manipulating me and his family who now did not want us back together either.

Almost four months after we separated, my husband and his sister came to visit me. They informed me that he did not want to get back to-gether any longer. He said that marriage counseling was for people who wanted to save their marriages, and he did not want to save our marriage. He said that his relationship with the Lord was just fine. He said that he did not want to stop drinking and smoking. Finally, he said that he did not want to stop talking to the other woman. His sister told me to leave him alone and get on with my life, the way that he was getting on with his. I knew that he had been lying to both of us. He had come to my house the day before wanting me to go to bed with him while I was baking cookies with all the kids in the neighborhood. My friend had even walked in and heard him calling my name to go to him. I had been rejecting him and his sexual advances and had made him angry again. Now, he and his sister (for backup) were confronting me and insisting that I get on with my life.

That night, for the first time, I decided to call a friend, the other woman's husband, who had called me and left me his number. He had told me to call him anytime. I just wanted to give him best wishes for a happy new year. However, his wife, the other woman, answered the phone. Within minutes, my phone was ringing with screaming and cursing again from my husband. He was extremely angry and threatening that I better not call them again or else. He threatened to severely hurt me if her husband touched her. Also, if I ever called them again, they would put a restraining order on me for harassing them.

I figured that she never even told her husband; she just called mine. I knew then that they were still secretly together and just waiting for the right time.

CHAPTER 14

Divorce

"Don't be afraid of what you are about to suffer. The devil will throw some of you into prison and put you to the test. You will be persecuted... Remain faithful even when facing death and I will give you the crown of life."
Revelation 2:10(NLT)

Divorce is never easy. Some people may think that once that decision is made to get divorced then everything should get easier. However, when you are dealing with a controlling and manipulative person, it is never easy to sever ties. The emotional and verbal abuse continues through the divorce process and in fact, it gives additional ammunition to use against the victim. Abusive people always blame others for any problems. Their personalities defy fault. They always feel that they are right and others are wrong. When a divorce is pending, the anger and resentment can be multiplied. It then makes the victim feel that they are being hit with a double-barrel blast of verbal and emotional attacks. Not only is the abuser verbally and emotionally attacking the victim again, but then the whole family gets in on the act to attack the person. Also, when a family knows no boundaries, the emotional and verbal abuse hits a new scale. The potential for violence increases. Fear can set in. When someone has witnessed illegal activities over years without any legal consequences, then who can protect that person? When certain people get away with unlawful activities routinely because they have close friends in law enforcement, then who is there to protect the innocent? The abuser is a liar and manipulator, so in most cases, he is laying his trap for disbelief of the victim. Even in the process of a divorce, the abusive person controls and manipulates those around him like playing a game of chess. In this situation, he gets set up for discrediting his victim. Fear can become overwhelming in a victim as events continue to occur around her with the abuser and the family. No one may be able to prove some things that occur, but she knows who is watching and waiting.

This is where my story continues again…

When a petition for divorce is obtained with child custody signed by the judge, there are court ordered behaviors that should be followed. When it says "no drinking in the presence of the children," then they should not be picked up by a drunken parent. When it says that the parent who has the children should not have a companion of the opposite sex spend the night, that rule should be followed. I received much harassment over these orders by the judge. I even got a recording of my husband stating that if he couldn't have his woman with him at night, he just wouldn't see his children. He would constantly lash out at me for so many things, but as we waited on the divorce to become finalized, my husband kept insisting on being friends "or else." His sister would continually come to my house asking who was there and what I was doing. She kept saying that I would always be family. My children would go over to her house frequently and were asked things about me. All that I did was work, go to church, take care of my children, and pray. However, more and more lies were being spread about me. His family was turning against me as more lies were told. His older brother would no longer look at me and kept accusing me of trying to kill his brother. Whenever his family was around, I could feel the difference in the way that my spouse treated me. When his brother was there, he was very mean and sarcastic. When his sister was there, he was very indifferent. However, when no one was watching, he was trying to be sweet and loving. He would still tell me that we may one day get back together. Again, I would keep insisting on the four things that I had demanded. I still loved him after all of those years of being together and despite all of the hurt. I saw what he was doing to manipulate everyone with his stories continuing to change, but I kept praying to God to change him. I also had our mutual friend witnessing both sides as an innocent bystander, knowing the truth.

More and more things were happening around my house. My storage shed was broken into multiple times. There were foot prints in the flowerbed beneath my bedroom window (after I heard a noise at the window the night before). My boat was damaged, requiring thousands of dollars of repairs. Even the owner of the marina told me that someone had vandalized my boat motor and that it was damaged by someone who knew what he were doing. He knew the family that I was dealing with and allowed my boat to stay at the marina free of charge to protect it. My generator was stolen from my carport. There were too many things happening to just be coincidence.

He was still insisting that we stay friends for the children. My children would come home after spending the weekend with their dad with stories of his drunkenness. He would not watch them, and they would get hurt in his yard. One son had a bad four-wheeler wreck where he said that he was lying on the ground with his breath knocked out of him. He said that his dad was drunk and just opened the door and yelled at him to come inside instead of going to check on him. The older teenage son was allowed to drink at his dad's house, and he received second and third degree burns to his leg while he played with his friends at a bonfire. He had told our youngest son, when he was only twelve years old, to bring two girls who were twins to his house to have sex with them in the bedroom. He also said to bring the girl's mother for him to have sex with her in his bedroom. I was not there to protect them any longer. They were living a life that I had tried to protect them from since they were born. Also, they were witnessing behaviors by their dad that were beyond my wildest imagination. I never thought that he would actually treat our own children that way. He was drinking, partying, playing, and at times, neglecting our children. He was failing as a parent, but I was getting all of the blame. Many times, the children would refuse to go to his house after talking to him. They could tell if he was drinking or angry already before they would even go to his house, and they would try to make excuses to not have to go to his house. Again, I was always getting the blame for the children not wanting to be with him. He could not see that his behavior was a huge problem. At times, he would beg me to go eat with the kids at his house. The children would usually want me to go, so at least I was there to protect them, and they would try to come home with me to sleep at our own house. Many times he would allow them to come home with me instead of staying there. I knew that his behavior was unstable, but deep down, I was still hoping and praying that he would snap out of whatever was wrong with him and change for the good of our family.

CHAPTER 15

The Death Threat

"He will rescue you again and again so that
no evil can touch you."
Job 5:19(NLT)

An abusive personality does not change overnight, especially when he/she doesn't even realize that they have a problem. People with that personality trait always tend to blame others for everything. They act irrationally, being very impulsive, and never consider consequences of their actions. It is very difficult to tell when an abusive person like this is close to exploding in anger again, because it can happen in a split second. They can be like time-bombs, and you never know for sure when they will explode. They can go from happy and laughing in one moment to angry and screaming in the next moment. Their pendulum of emotions can swing back and forth like a yoyo that goes up and down. That is why it is so hard to judge when it is safe around someone like that. The angry stage varies from fussing, cussing, yelling, screaming, cursing, threatening, swinging, hitting, and etc.

It seems that it should be so easy to walk away from a relationship like that, but it is so difficult. When an abusive person like that has had years of emotional torment on another person, that victim always fears the worst and knows the potential for harm. What seems like simple warnings in joking to other people on the outside, really mean a whole lot more to the victim living in the situation. The old saying that "You don't know what happens behind closed doors" is so true for abuse. Law enforcement needs more education to identify the warning signs and identify who is being truthful and who is not. A life may depend on it.

My story continues here…

This is not easy for me to write. I was the one there. I was the victim. After the divorce was final, I continued to try to remain friends as he demanded. He would invite me to his house with the kids to barbeque for supper on his weekends. Our families did not know. He kept telling me that he loved me and hoped that we could eventually get back together as a family. I kept telling him that the kids and I had to trust him. There were times that I could tell he was so angry, but he would be under control. There were other times that I could not even tell that there was a problem till something happened. The first incident happened several weeks after the divorce was finalized.

He had a mobile home and land in the country, and we would all ride four wheelers around his property. One night, he decided to burn a big pile of uprooted trees, trash, bushes, and overgrowth that remained in his yard from when the property had been cleared prior to him purchasing it. It was about 30 to 40 feet in diameter, and he could not see or walk in it because it was so thick with uprooted trees and overgrowth. He actually had no idea what was in the middle of this pile. Initially he poured gasoline over most of it, and then started lighting fires around the pile. He almost caught his own leg on fire as he carelessly stood on the fire. Again, he was drinking. Since the pile was so big, he decided that we would ride the four wheelers around the pile to make sure that the grass would not catch on fire. There was a tremendous amount of heat put off as this fire burned down. Our ten year old daughter was riding on the four-wheeler with us as we went around monitoring the flames. Suddenly, he drove right for the fire and put the front tire in the fire. My daughter and I were screaming for him to stop and move from the fire. He kept saying that he would not get closer, and he kept saying that the tires were fire proof. We were both screaming to get away from the fire, and we jumped off the four-wheeler. He told us that we were both crazy. He kept encouraging us to get back on, and he said that he would not go near the fire.

My daughter refused to get back on the four-wheeler, and she begged me not to, but I blindly or stupidly got back on the four-wheeler, despite my ten-year-old daughter pleading with me not to trust him. Immediately, he drove right for the fire with us screaming as loud as we could. I could hear my daughter scream and cry even over my own screams and the sound of the engine as he drove me very slowly over the huge pile of debris on fire. The heat was intense. I kept wanting to jump off but had sandals on, and I knew that I would get severely burnt. He had no idea if this pile would collapse because he could never get into it, much less ride over it. My daughter was hysterical as she watched her parents slowly ride over a huge pile of debris on fire. I was physically ill from screaming and crying. When we finally got over the burning pile, I told him that he had a death wish, and he was trying to take me with him. He just laughed at me. Then, I told him that it was like being raped. He angrily turned around to look at me and in this evil voice and with a look of almost hatred, he said that I did not know what it felt like to be raped. I knew that he did not remember what he had done to me years before. My daughter and I went into the house crying. I went into the bathroom, crumpled on the floor, and vomited and cried uncontrollably. My fear had just taken a new level. His neighbor heard the intense screaming and came over to see if everything was OK! He just told her we were having fun in the backyard!

Now, I was even more afraid. I had been victim to what I knew was a death threat. He didn't verbalize it, but I knew that what I told him was accurate. He had a death wish and wanted to take me with him. Then, he was cruel enough to have our child watch! She was terrified of him. She no longer wanted to go visit him. I cried and cried for days. I had witnessed a new level of cruelty to me and my child. I tried to tell his family that something was wrong, but they just laughed. I told my family, and they told me to stay away from him. My family felt that he had been trying to injure me or even kill me. God had protected me despite my stupidity.

He continued to call me every day, and I kept trying to pull away. I was trying to get control over my own life; however, he still had a control over me. I was very afraid of him and his behavior. I had been feeling that his anger was increasing as I was refusing to talk to him or be with him. I finally decided to get the courage to try to talk to him. I needed to tell him how I felt. I needed to try to talk some sense into him for him to get help. He insisted that I go to his house to talk. I began shaking and crying as I drove up in his yard. I had been traumatized again by that last event. I tried to tell him that I was afraid of him and that I really thought that he had tried to kill me; but the words would not come out. I was terrified of him! He was still in control! He led me into his bathroom as I was crying and trembling. There, he had a large tub full of bath water ready. He undressed me and made me get in the tub despite my pleading to stop and just talk as I continued to cry. I kept saying that I needed to just talk to him. He repeatedly told me to "shut up and stop crying" because it was a "turn off," and it was making him mad. I cried the entire time as he bathed me, telling me to stop crying. I was getting more terrified because I could not stop crying and shaking. He kept saying louder and louder that it was making him mad, and he was getting obviously angry. He finished and insisted on drying me off, despite me telling him that I could do it. Again, he led me to his bed and had sex with me as I cried continually, telling him no. He repeatedly told me to "stop crying" because it was "turning him off." He kept saying that I was making him mad. He started yelling at me and demanding that I make noises so he would know that he was "doing me some good." I was laying there as he had sex with me. He was biting me and hurting me as I cried. I tried telling him to stop and that he was hurting me, but he would not stop. He had also recently started chasing me around the house and biting me hard on my buttocks which would leave bruises on my body. He then demanded that I like it when I insisted that I didn't and that he was hurting me. At that moment at his house, he was doing what he wanted and yelling for me to "kiss him like I meant it." Then he demanded that I say that "I loved him like I meant it." I was terrified and crying the entire time. It was at that moment that I realized that my love for that man was being destroyed by him. He would not take "NO" for an answer. He would not listen to me. He had absolute and total control over me. I was a rag doll in his hands. He finished and rolled off of me. I told him that I had to get home and left. We did absolutely no talking. I went home crying and feeling so filthy. I felt like I had been raped again! I had been used again by that man! I could not stand up to him! I felt so dirty and so cheap! How could I have let that man do that to me? I jumped in the shower to wash him off of me and then just lay in bed crying all night long. I had to stay away from him! I had to break that control that he had over me. I was even more terrified of him now!

I prayed everyday that God would move me and my kids away or bring me joy right where I was. I realized that that man had total control over me. I was like a fish on a line that he just reeled in whenever he wanted me. I had never been able to stand up to him or defend myself from him. I was trying to pull away from him and like a fish on a fishing line, he would keep fighting to reel me back in. I was seeing more and more anger in him when I talked to him. I knew that I could not go back to his house; his domain was where the last two episodes of total violation and abuse had occurred.

My children did not want to leave that area. That was their hometown where they were born and their friends were living. So, I contacted a contractor to build a new house for my kids and me so we could move away from his family. The new house was begun almost two months after my divorce was final. I did not tell him that I was definitely going to build a new house until the work was started. I was afraid that he would harass me and talk me out of it. He and his sister had sat on my front porch and told me to get on with my life. I had been trying to do that but he still had a hold on me. He kept reeling me back into his life. I was trying to break that control over me. However, I kept seeing him get angrier and angrier when I did not want to talk to him or see him. When I finally told him that construction on a new house was started, he was extremely angry. He liked us right where we were—next to his sister's house where everyone could watch us.

Later that day, I went to visit some old friends—the first couple that lived next to us when we first got married. I told them everything that had been going on with his increase in anger and violence. I told them that I was trying to get my life together and move from him and his family. They both told me that they needed to tell me some things. I cried uncontrollably as they told me story after story of the abuse that they had witnessed with their own eyes and heard as they lived near us. They informed me that they could hear him yelling at me through the mobile home walls.

They gave me many examples of mean, hateful things that he had told me over the years, and they both said that I would not answer back or defend myself. They told me that they quit inviting us over or visiting because of his drinking and abusive behavior. They also told me about his partying at bars and sexual affairs with two women that occurred as I was working various shifts to support him when he took leave from work and went to college after we were only married a few years. They told me about how he used me to buy new vehicle after new vehicle. They said that they constantly would ask him why and his response to them was that his wife was a nurse, and he could afford whatever he wanted—in fact, he did not even have to work! They told me that they always feared that he would bankrupt us with his excessive spending. I tearfully told them that he had accused me of being controlling with money and abusive to him. They said that if I had not tried to reason with him to save some money, that he would have broken us financially. They knew about him changing careers from a high paying job to a minimum paying policeman job immediately after the birth of our third child and also commented about his irrational and selfish decisions which affected us as a family. They also told me that they had repeatedly watched as I silently let him emotionally and verbally abuse me. It was the first time that someone was telling me what they had witnessed from the beginning of our marriage and that I had been abused and even used financially. They told me that they could no longer stand to watch as my children and I were verbally and emotionally abused, and amazingly, we didn't even realize it. They backed out of our lives to protect their own family. My loving friends were standing beside me then and witnessed what went on every day, even since the divorce. He started calling me again and again repeatedly.

The calls were continuous. Normally, I would answer almost immediately because he would get mad if I didn't. This time, I just let it ring and ring as I cried beside my long-time friends. My ex-husband would still call multiple times a day, and then he would tell his family that I was calling him. Call after call after endless call came, but this time, I did not answer. My friend's husband finally answered the phone for me. He told my ex-husband to leave me alone. He told him to quit calling me. He told my ex that they had watched me be abused for years by him and that it was enough! He told him that he was telling me all of the truth about all those years. I listened as my friend defended me as he talked to my ex. When he got off the phone, he told me that I needed to go hide out in a motel room for a couple of days. I told him no and that I would go home with my children. He told me that my ex was very angry and that he perceived a threat—he was told that <u>the best thing that could happen was for me to be dead!</u> We talked for a long time as years of incidences were recounted for me. They had watched even from a distance and knew everything that had been going on for years. People recognized the abuse when I couldn't even see it. They told me the truth that day instead of the lies that I had been led to believe for years. I went home even more determined to get on with my life.

Later that evening, I went to my contractor's house to meet with them while my oldest son stayed with the other kids. As I was there, my cell phone started ringing and ringing again. I kept canceling the calls, but the calls kept coming. I finally answered it and heard screaming and cursing. He called me so many horrible names and made multiple threats about taking the kids. I kept hanging up on him, and he kept calling back. I left to go home while crying hysterically. He told me that if I hung up on him again, he would kill me. He was calling from his house phone initially where he had no cell service. I took off in a panic to go home. He kept calling; this time he was calling from his cell phone so I knew that he was on the way. At first he was breaking up from bad reception and as he got closer, his call was clearer and clearer. I knew that he was on his way and getting nearer. He told me that he was on his way to kill me. He said that he had a gun, and he was going to shoot me and then himself. I knew that he had an arsenal of guns, and I knew that he was very capable of violence. I rushed home, calling my friends that had supported me that day. They refused to help, telling me that they knew that he was crazy, and they had to protect their own children. They told me to call the police! I rushed home and told the kids to pack some clothes. I called the police and told them that I had been threatened. I told them that he was on his way to kill me. A policeman, who was my ex's buddy, drove up at my house. My ex-sister-in-law came over too. I told them the story. My sister-in-law told the police that I would not leave him alone—that I was always calling him and harassing him. She told him that her brother was trying to get on with his life, and I would not let go. The police officer called my ex-husband on his phone. He laughingly told me that my ex had only gone to a store for gasoline then was innocently going home. He had denied everything! The police officer, who knew us both but worked with my ex, sided with him. He told me to leave my ex alone and get on with my life. He told me to stop calling my ex. I tried to tell them that he was calling me, but they all believed him. I was again made to look like a fool by his scheming lies.

Everyone left, and my kids and I were alone again with the doors locked. My phone started ringing and ringing again, but I would not answer it. He would not stop calling. Then, he called our son's cell phone. I had told our son to always answer our calls. My son handed me the phone when his dad told him that he wanted to talk to me. I finally answered it to hear a voice that I had never heard before. I had heard many threats before, but this one was different. This one was so very real!!! It was so low pitched and evil! My children were beside me as I cried and listened in shock. His speech was very slow, dragging out each word in a deliberate, deep threat! It sounded so demonic. He told me,

"Oh, now you have done it!! Now you have done it!! You have managed to turn all of our old friends against me… and now you are turning my coworkers against me… Oh, now you have done it!!! …It may not be today…. It may not be tomorrow… But, you better watch over your shoulders!!! One of these days, when you least expect it, I WILL KILL YOU!!!"

He went on and on with horrible threats, telling me how he would enjoy watching me suffer. I was frozen in shock. I just kept crying in fear as he slowly, evilly told me that he was going to kill me and take my children. My sixteen year old son grabbed the phone from my hands and turned it off. He took control as his mother was speechless and in shock. He grabbed me and our stuff as well as the other kids, loaded us up in the vehicle, and took off. We took off so quickly that we forgot the dog. When we went back to get the dog, my ex-sister-in-law was standing in the driveway. Her brother was calling and calling her and trying to reach us. She begged me to talk to her brother. He called my cell phone as we drove away with the dog to go to my family several hours away. I just sat and listened as he talked. He did not even realize that we were in our car and leaving the area with my son driving to safety. Now, he was being remorseful.

He told me that after all of those years, he had to admit to me that I had been right. He told me that he lied to the marriage counselors and that he never wanted to go to counseling. He also told me that counseling did not do him any good because he was smarter than the counselors. He said that he just told the counselors what they wanted to hear. He admitted to me that he was very smart and finally told me that he was a genius with an IQ over 140. He said that he knew how to manipulate people. He told me that he knew exactly what people wanted to hear and would tell them just that. He also told me that he could manipulate anyone.

Everything that I had suspected over all those years, he acknowledged in that one phone call. I knew that he was very smart. I knew that his stories were frequently not exactly the same, but then he would repeatedly say that I was stupid and could never remember what he told me. He repeatedly lied to me and others, changing his stories or saying exactly what he knew that they wanted to hear. But, as an abuser, he would yell and scream and criticize me and call me stupid and crazy for not remembering things. Also, as a victim, I repeatedly blamed myself for not remembering everything that he would claim that he told me. He had finally admitted what I had suspected all of those years and especially since we had split. He was a master manipulator and could manipulate anyone, just like he manipulated his family, his police officer friends, and former counselors. He had finally admitted it to me! I knew that he could not be trusted. My phone died as he continued to talk while I just listened to long awaited confessions. I knew that I needed to get some help to protect me from this man.

CHAPTER 16

Getting Help

"My help comes from the Lord, who made the heavens and the earth! He will not let you stumble and fall; the one who watches over you will not sleep. Indeed, He who watches over you never tires and never sleeps. The Lord himself watches over you!"
Psalm 121:2-5 (NLT)

There are many women across this nation and in this world that are affected by abusive people and situations. To an outsider, it seems that it would be so easy to just walk away or to avoid the situation all together to begin with. However, manipulative people who abuse others are really so cunning and secretive, that they manage to scheme their way into the hearts of these innocent, unsuspecting women. Sometimes, it seems like a person with low self-esteem becomes a magnet for these abusive people. An unsuspecting person will not think that they are being tricked. When someone is truthful and honest, they expect others to be truthful and honest. That is their nature. However, these people can easily become a target for those with abusive tendencies. It is also their nature to try to please everyone. After years of abuse, they feel inadequate and want to fix everything. Unfortunately, most abusive people are never totally happy and pleasing them becomes an impossible task.

The victims of these abusers are actually under a type of bondage to their abusers—an emotional bondage and spiritual bondage. Some people call them "soul ties". These "soul ties" have to be broken for the victim to move on and for healing to begin. When a person lives in constant fear of emotional, verbal and physical attacks, their responses to words and actions are so different than someone without these fears. Outsiders may think that these people are crazy to live with the constant abuse, but they are almost stuck in that situation until they get help to get out of it. It is a battle to break these "soul ties"—an emotional battle, a spiritual battle, and even a physical battle. The attacks get more and more vicious as the abuser feels that they are losing control. The abusive person always wants to stay in control of any situation. Their grasp gets tighter and tighter, harder and harder as they feel that they are losing their grip on the situation. They are determined to show that they are superior, and they will do whatever it takes to keep their dominance over their victim. That is why the abusive eruptions and explosions get more and more frequent and more severe when a victim is trying to break away, almost like labor pains when a woman is giving birth. It is actually like a birth process—the birth of freedom for someone who has lived under bondage of abuse.

The first step to take when a victim is threatened and fears for her life is to get to safety. The initial safety may be with family or friends. In some cases it may be with the police. Some police may need more education to identify warning signs to abuse. Just because they know both parties does not mean that they know what goes on behind closed doors. From a safety area, the next thing to do is to contact the local woman's shelter. The local woman's shelter may be someone's first safe haven if there are no families or friends. Most shelters are very secure to provide safety to those who are there for protection already, so they may not just open their doors at any time of the night. The police should be the first line of defense in that situation. The women's shelters provide counseling, food, clothing, lodging, and legal assistance to all women and children who are victims of abuse. Their legal procedures work expediently with the court system to get the legal protection that these women and children need during these situations. These women all need the counseling services to help them emotionally and to help them relearn behaviors. All women's shelters services are free to anyone in need regardless of financial status.

This is where my story continues again…

I knew that this death threat was very real. I heard it in his voice, not once but twice, with both calls. I knew that he was on his way to kill me and that he was physically capable. I knew that he said that one day he would do it when I least expected it. I knew that he had wanted me dead when he took me over that fire. I knew that he had wanted to hurt me when he took me in the jeep. I knew that he never took no for an answer. I knew that he had told our friend that day that the best thing was for me to be dead. I knew that for years he had talked about killing me and making it look like I ran off or that it was an accident. All of these thoughts whirled around my head as my son drove me and my other children to safety. We had to go north to get to my family, and he lived north of our location so by him staying on the phone talking, he did not know that we were leaving the area. He thought that we were still home. I was still in shock, not speaking, but listening to him being truthful for the first time about his lies, manipulations, and scheming. He knew that he had crossed the line. My phone died just north of his location, so we were in a safe zone heading toward my family. My family waited up for us to arrive and listened to the entire story. They had seen his abuse of me over the years and had been praying for me. They knew that his death threat was real. My children knew that it was real. My oldest son took over as a protector and became a man beyond his sixteen years that very moment. When I could not think for being in a state of shock, he took over and made very adult decisions. My family and I had to get together and make a plan. I needed help. I could not do this alone.

The next day, we contacted the local women's shelter in the area that we lived. I also contacted my attorney from my recent divorce who gave me advice. As soon as I charged my phone and turned it on that day, the phone started ringing and ringing again. I finally answered it and told him to leave me alone. He was so apologetic and begged me not to file charges. He was now a special education teacher and was fearful of losing his job. He told me that he tried calling my house and phone all night long. I told him again to just leave me alone. I hung up and turned the phone off again. I immediately had my cell phone number changed. Later that day, my son drove us back the two hours distance to our house. I went immediately to the women's shelter. My ex was a former police officer, and his former coworkers believed him. I felt that I did not have protection in our city due to their response to my complaints the night before. At the Women's Shelter, I told them the entire story about the death threats, his drinking, and increasing explosive behaviors. The legal advocate there immediately went to the court house and obtained a Protective Order signed by the judge. My ex could not come within 300 feet of me. He could not even legally go to his sister's house which was two doors down from mine. He and his entire family were mad at me. They repeatedly stated that I was blowing things out of proportion and that he did not mean it. They all defended him. I was called the mean one and crazy one again.

There was one police officer/ detective and his family who were friends with me and my kids. They believed me. They tried to help protect me and my children. My children had told them that they were afraid of him at times. They had seen him get angry and yell uncontrollably at our oldest son. They had heard the truth from the children as well as from me. The city police department was given a copy of the Protective Order the very day that it was signed by the judge. A few days later, my children and I were at the home of this police officer and his family. There was a banging on the front door, and his daughter yelled that it was my ex. The officer told me and his wife to stay hidden in the backyard while he took care of it. My ex was demanding to see me and talk to me. He kept saying that he needed to see me. This officer told him that there was a protective order protecting me from him and that he could not come near me. My ex angrily stated that he had not been served yet! The officer told him, "Consider yourself served!" and told him to get off his property and stay away from me. He had witnessed the anger and demanding nature of my ex as he protected me. This officer later followed me and the children home to make sure that we got there safely. He and his wife and family were supporters of my children and me during our time of turmoil. They were some of the few who knew the truth and saw through the lies and manipulations of my ex and his family.

A few weeks after the Protective Order was issued, I was in the storage shed in my backyard with my daughter and a neighbor. He was trying to help me put a new lock on my door because it had been broken into again. When we walked into the yard, I heard a bunch of noise coming from inside my house. I looked in the driveway and saw my ex-husband's vehicle parked there. He must have been hitting walls as he went through the house. I heard him walk out of the back door of my house. My neighbor left. I told my ex that I had a protective order and that he was not supposed to be near me, much less in my house. I asked him what he was doing there. He yelled, "So that's who you are fxxxing!" I told him that the neighbor was helping us change the lock. He screamed "No!" then named the detective friend who had helped me that day while his wife and I hid in the backyard. He angrily screamed to me and our daughter that it was my entire fault. Everything was my fault! He was yelling that I was having sex with the detective. He also yelled for me to call him to come over and watch what would happen to him. He was threatening to hurt the detective who had helped us. He was yelling about getting in trouble with his boss and possibly losing his job. He was blaming me for the protective order and saying that I blew everything out of proportion. He read the entire legal papers to my daughter as he yelled and screamed at me. He kept yelling that everything was my fault. My other children and their friend (the detective's son) arrived and were met with cursing and yelling. He lied and told that young man that his dad and I were having sex and that was why he sided with me. He told my children lies about me having sex with any man that tried to help me, including the neighbor that had just left and several others. He was angrily yelling and telling lies about me as my children and I all just stood frozen under the carport and cried as he continued on his rampage.

He then told us that he was moving to Europe with a friend of his (a female teacher). He told our children that they would never see him again. Needless to say, my children and I were all crying and upset witnessing this wild, explosive behavior. I begged him not to do this to our children. Their dad took off, yelling and screaming, in his vehicle, going toward his sister's house. We were all crying, standing in my carport and in shock again. My sons and their friend took off crying in his vehicle. I went into the house through the carport door for the first time since I saw my ex on my property. Someone knocked on my front door. I opened it to find my ex-sister-in-law there. She was asking me what was going on. Before I could say much, three police cars speedily drove up. They jumped out of their vehicles and hurried to my house. They told her to leave and for me to get into the house. They started questioning me about what had happened. I told them the entire story. They kept asking me if I had invited him in, and I kept denying it. He was in my house when I walked out of my storage shed! They kept asking me question after question. I told them about the neighbor being there and seeing him. I even asked them if the neighbor had called the police since all of my neighbors knew that I had a protective order. They were interrogating me like I had committed a crime. I did not understand what was going on! I could not get in contact with my sons. This detective/police officer's son was with my sons and had just heard my ex lie to him that his dad and I were having sex. I felt so overwhelmed again. I finally asked them again before they left, "Who called the police?" I thought one of the neighbors had called. The detective told me that he was at home when he got a call at home from my family—my sister. He said that I must have called my sister. I told him that I never got to a phone because we were outside and the phone was inside the house. He said that a neighbor must have called her. The detective stated that he got a call from my sister who was two hours away and was hysterical. He said that she was screaming,

"He is in the house and he is there to kill her!!"

He said that he jumped into his car and called for backup as he raced to my home. All three police cars got to my house right after my ex had left my property. The detective thought that either I or a neighbor had called her to call him since my family had his phone number in case they needed to get in touch with me or my children. I kept denying that I had called anyone. Everything had happened too fast for me to call anyone for help…

After the police left, I called my sister. I was crying. My daughter was crying. I still could not get in contact with my sons. My sister was very upset. She was asking me if I was ok. I asked her if a neighbor had called her. She said no. I kept asking her how did she find out...How did she know that my ex was in my house?????

She finally told me,

"I was in the shower and the Lord told me clearly in an audible voice—

'HE IS IN THE HOUSE... AND HE IS THERE TO KILL HER!'

CHAPTER 17

Legal Battles

"The Lord gives righteousness and justice to all who are treated unfairly."
Psalm 103:6(NLT)

Many times, an abused person feels that they will never have a moment of peace. After a death threat, many are constantly on the look-out, constantly looking over their shoulder. It is normal for women like this to be very fearful. Any noise outside or inside of the house brings a response of fear. Any sound of anger brings a knee jerk reaction of fear. The victim in this situation may fear going out in public and may constantly watch out for their abuser or his family. They are always in a flight mode, ready to leave an area in the first sign of trouble. They tend to jump if someone comes up behind them or touches them from the back. They may cry easily. They may avoid crowds. They may have difficulty sleeping. They may have recurrent nightmares. They may drive through parking lots watching for certain vehicles and leave if they think that their abuser may be there. They may be constantly watching over their shoulders and living in fear. They are in a constant state of alert. This is a normal response to a death threat. The victim may have a similar response to those soldiers in a war who experience post-traumatic stress. The victim has actually been in her own type of war involving people that she has loved. This adds wounds to someone who has already been one of "the walking wounded."

It is very important when someone is in this type of situation to continue to get legal assistance. A Protective Order is one of the most powerful protections that can be obtained besides protective custody. However, it is still only written on paper and is only good for the law abiding citizen who does not want to break the law. With a Protective Order, the assailant can not have guns in their possession and must keep a long distance from their victim. It is meant to protect the victim from further harassment and harm. The Women's Shelters provide legal assistance also when any Protective Order is broken which is still free to any woman in need.

It is also very important for the victim to continue with counseling for her and her children. Any death threat is an emotional and verbal assault and can be very damaging to the victim and children. Many people may think that such threats should be easily "blown off" but to the victim, it is very real and a possibility that she lives with daily. Some may say that the abuser did not mean it or he was just angry. However, the victim has been the one who has been emotionally and verbally and even physically beat down over years—she knows that he really meant it. By this time, the victim knows that the abuser is capable of carrying out his threat. This death threat is very real, and the victim constantly lives with that threat in her head.

This is where my story continues again…

My divorce attorney as well as the Women's Shelter's attorney joined forces to help me during this emotional time. I was so confused. There was a court hearing during this time right after the Protective Order was issued and then broken. My ex did not bring an attorney. The judge was talking to him about the charges and that he needed an attorney. My ex continued to argue with the judge saying that it was not his fault and that he could not afford an attorney. The judge told him to get an attorney. My ex kept trying to talk to me. My family and attorneys would keep me away from him. I was so scared of him that I kept trying to listen to what he had to say. Finally, my attorney from the Women's Shelter cornered me. She told me that she had been doing this for over 10 years and that she could see right through my ex. She said that she could tell that he was a manipulator. She said that she could tell from the way that he spoke to the judge that he was abusive to me. She then threatened me with a reciprocal restraining order. She said that if I even let him get near me to talk to me that she would issue a restraining order against me to stay away from him to protect me and my children. She said that it was very obvious that he had a control over me, and I had to stay away from him.

My attorneys kept checking on the charges from the district attorney's office for when he broke the protective order by being in my house. Initially, they were told that there was not enough evidence to pursue charges. Remember, my ex-husband was an ex police officer and that city's police force did the paperwork. My attorneys continued to question this considering the fact that I had a neighbor that witnessed that he was in my house without me knowing it and that I had not invited him into my house. The DA's office finally accepted charges against him then, and he finally got an attorney to represent him.

The emotional turmoil continued as his family who lived two doors down was very angry with me. My ex-husband even left a message on my voice mail one day saying that he knew that he was breaking the Protective Order but wanted to talk to me. He said that he was angry but would have never hurt me and that he was sorry. I knew that this man knew no boundaries. I brought this recording to my attorney. His family kept calling me and begging me to call him. I was also trying to sell my house at that time to move away from his family, just waiting for my new house to be completed. My realtor was getting harassing phone calls about my house day and night. She would get calls with blocked numbers saying negative things about my house. Harassing calls to her about the asking price were coming daily. She would get calls with people obviously disguising their voices with "made-up" names and asking question after question about my house. She told me that she had never experienced behavior like this with any house that she had ever put on the market. She felt that they were calls from my ex and his family.

My ex was not able to go to his sister's house due to the Protective Order. He could talk to the children, but he could only see them at a court ordered safe house for child visitation for protection. His family was angry and was telling the children that I was sending their dad to jail. This was all emotional abuse to my children. He would meet his family at his nephew's house which was a block over. One day, his vehicle was at his sister's house for several days. I finally called the police department to just check since I had the Protective Order. I later found out that he had been admitted to a psychiatric unit for attempted suicide. My friend and her husband, who was still my ex sister-in-law's best friend, would visit me and keep me updated on the craziness that went on over there. He had a new girlfriend, and he had everyone believing that I was the mean one. He had them believing that I had lied or exaggerated everything, and I had purposefully turned the children against him. Now everyone was angry with me for his attempted suicide. It just proved to me that he was capable of violence—whether against me or himself.

His brother-in-law called my children one day to tell them that he was coming over to get anything in the storage shed that belonged to my ex. I left work and met them at my house. He was very angry and kept saying that I had destroyed my ex-husband. He kept saying that I had done this to my ex. I kept trying to tell him about the ride over the burning bonfire and the death threats and that I feared for my life. I said that I knew that he really meant it. His comment was that my ex had been drinking and did not mean it. The entire family was very mad and blaming me for his attempted suicide. In their minds, he was blameless; it was my entire fault. I knew that these people always sought revenge, and I was afraid.

One day at the end of that summer, I received a call from my youngest son while I was at work. He was very upset and told me that he and a friend had just walked in on his uncle involved in an oral sex act with an employee in his place of business. My son was afraid and said that his uncle, just two doors down, kept calling him to go over. He was terrified. I called my ex-brother-in-law and told him to leave my son alone. I told him to not call my house any more. He asked me what my son said, and I responded that he knew good and well what he was doing. I told him to leave me and my children alone. I rushed home to find my son and his friend barricaded in my bedroom with every door locked and holding a shot gun. He was terrified, and he said that his uncle kept calling him, getting more and more upset, and that he felt that he was coming after him. He said that his uncle was cursing and yelling at him and my son was afraid that he would try to hurt him. I had called my friend in the neighborhood from work, who was still my ex-sister-in-law's best friend. I had cried as I told her the story. She knew that I was being truthful. She also came over later and heard the story from my young son, who was only 13 years old at that time. She told my ex-sister-in-law the truth after my ex-brother-in-law told his wife that I was spreading lies about him. This friend had repeatedly told my ex-sister-in-law the truth as she witnessed what was actually happening and the constant lies that were spoken about me.

My ex-in-laws got into a big fight the next day about his affair that he was having with an employee. He got angry and assaulted his wife. The police were called. When the police came, they found crystal meth, drug paraphernalia, marijuana plants, lots of cash, etc. We all knew that he was into smoking pot, but we had never known the extent of their illegal activities until that day. My son never went home alone again! He was terrified! I had to make arrangements for him to go to a friend's house after school till I could pick him up. My children and I all knew the potential for violence with that family. We had witnessed it and heard many stories of illegal activities from others who reported things to the police, but nothing was ever done regarding their reports. My attorney was notified of all of these events and began trying to protect my children as well as myself. Multiple state and then federal charges were reportedly filed against my ex- brother-in-law as his illegal activities were investigated. My ex-in-laws split up, and my ex-brother-in-law was very mad at me and my son. Again, we were living in fear. We only lived two doors from them and would not put anything past them. We did not trust them.

My children and I continued to go to our counselors with all of the turmoil going on in our lives. I even went to the support group at the women's shelter. I had so much compared to these other woman—I had a job, a house, a vehicle, my children, a new house under construction, finances; but I was living in constant fear. I was an emotional wreck. I was afraid to go to the grocery store in case I ran into him or his family. I was crying frequently. I was constantly looking over my shoulder everywhere that I went. I was having nightmares. My children and I were aware of the known "wild side" of his family and their lawlessness. For his family to be that angry with me brought more fear to me. Many people were aware of their frequent illegal activities and their ability to not get caught or have any consequences for their actions. One son would try to get in contact with his dad, but their dad would frequently not answer their calls. I was trying to provide emotional support to my own children but was emotionally drained. His family was all mad at me. My realtor continued to get harassing phone calls about my house.

My contractor was continuing work on my new house. I kept feeling like I was in a whirlwind again with all of the turmoil going on around me and my children. I could not understand why I was so overwhelmed. Every counselor, for my children and me, was telling us to move away. But, my children did not want to leave the area where they had grown up. My family was still two hours away. I had many friends, but I felt so alone. I just continued to pray for guidance and protection.

My family prayed for me and my children daily. They had seen the abuse and knew the volatile potential of my ex and his family. I continued to turn to the Lord to help me and guide me through every day. I kept going to a Spirit-filled church and growing closer to God. I knew that He was watching over me. I knew that He had sent help for me. I knew that God did not lie and that he told my sister that my ex was in the house to kill me. The Lord knows everyone's heart. It did not matter what my ex-husband said. I had heard it from the Lord exactly what his intent was that day. My sister was over 100 miles away when she called the police. I remembered a year before when I was praying with my sister on the phone that she told me that Jesus just told her that He was in the room with me. I had opened my eyes to see Jesus looking down at me. I still did not realize how much God was protecting me. I did not even believe that I was worthy of God's help. I kept praying for the Lord to forgive me for ever marrying that man and marrying into his family. I kept praying for Him to protect me and my children. I also kept praying for my children and me to be able to forgive that whole family for all that they had done to hurt us. I also realized that they did not even realize that they had hurt us. They all felt that I was the one that hurt them.

I was living in such fear at the time that I wrote a detailed letter describing those death threats and the intense fear that I was living in. I felt that I was being stalked and feared for my life. I wrote what could be considered my "will" giving my oldest brother and sister control over my estate and requesting that my family have custody of my children if something happened to me. I had it notarized and gave copies to my attorney, a friend, and my counselor. I had requested that if something happened to me, that my ex-husband and his family be investigated. I knew that they had friends in law enforcement, had been able to get away with many illegal activities, and that my ex had told me for years that he could kill me and no one would ever know what happened to me. I had seen his anger. I had experienced his violence. I felt that most people thought that I was crazy because that was what he was telling everyone. I needed someone to believe me and protect my children if something happened to me.

CHAPTER 18

The Perfect Storm

"When your terror comes like a storm and your
destruction comes like a whirlwind, when distress and
anguish come upon you, Then they will call on Me..."
Proverbs 1:27-28 (NKJV)

An abused person lives in an emotional whirlwind during various periods of his/her life. When people are already overwhelmed with the current events in their lives, their tolerance for more traumas is very low. Even the simplest little event can send them reeling into an emotional "basketcase" again. To an abused person who is in a point in his/her live that they are living on edge or in fear, any change in the routine is overwhelming again and can send them "over the edge". What some people would think is simple or not important can be a major occurrence to someone who is already totally "stressed out". An example would be similar to a rubber band that may be stretched to its maximum capacity. If even the slightest increase in tension is placed on that rubber band, it will pop. The final movement may be ever so slight or barely noticeable, but it is that final motion that will cause it to break.

There are several kinds of whirlwinds that can exist in a person's life. Not only are there emotional whirlwinds, but there are spiritual and physical whirlwinds. A person can be in a spiritual whirlwind or spiritual battle with all kinds of the turmoil surrounding them. This spiritual battle involves good versus evil or right versus wrong. Then, there are also physical whirlwinds. It may be a personal whirlwind like a physical attack on a person or it may be an environmental whirlwind with property damage. Either way, these can be very traumatic to people.

During the summer of 2005, the Gulf Coast was hit with two major hurricanes, Hurricane Katrina and then Hurricane Rita. Many people's lives were affected by these two traumatic events. It seemed that the Gulf Coast was almost wiped out. In fact, parts of the Gulf Coast have never been the same since. Many people have never returned to their homes or cities. Many of these people had no home to return to because their homes were destroyed. Thousands of people were displaced. The Mississippi Coastline was destroyed. Millions of people watched in horror on television as the poor victims of Hurricane Katrina sat for days at the Super Dome awaiting rescue and many victims clung to rooftops awaiting rescue. There were bodies floating in the flooded streets of New Orleans. Survivors were sent all over the southern states to safety. Then, Hurricane Rita hit. Evacuees from Hurricane Katrina became evacuees from Hurricane Rita. People were in a state of panic with all of the emotional and physical turmoil going on. Families were separated during this dreadful summer with these two monster hurricanes. Many lives were changed forever during this period of time.

Again, this is where my story continues…

My children and I had already lived through more emotional whirlwinds than the normal person during the past several years. I had survived several personal attacks physically, but emotionally, I was still living in fear like a person with PTSD—Post Traumatic Stress Disorder. We were still living in a spiritual whirlwind with a constant battle between right and wrong. I was still being constantly lied about and blamed for many things that were not my fault. Friends were even under attack just for helping me. They had nails in their tires, glass bottles being thrown in their driveways, pellet or BB shots to their vehicles and houses. My real estate agent was still getting harassing calls. They all reported to me that they knew where they were coming from but had no proof. I was in the process of building a new house and selling another. I had to move from that neighborhood! I had a Protective Order to protect me and my children, but that did not stop the feeling of fear. The Protective Order had already been broken once with him in my house and once with a phone call. His family was calling and begging me to call him. Now the entire family was even angrier. My ex-sister-in-law would tell my children that I was sending their dad to jail. The children were upset. I was even more upset. I could not stop the feeling that I was being stalked.

My house was sold for even more than we were asking. The harassing calls even increased to my realtor when word got out how much I was getting for the house—over $30,000 more than any house in that neighborhood had ever sold for. I knew that this was a blessing from God. The children and I were packed up and getting ready to move into the upstairs bedrooms of our new house while construction continued. I was scheduled to sign the papers to sell the house when we had to evacuate our area due to the hurricane. We evacuated to safety to where my family lived. The southern part of our state was out of electricity for weeks. My children and I lived between family members during this time. It was between 3 and 4 weeks before we could return to our home with electricity for me to return to work. Emotionally, I was exhausted. I had cried many tears again during this period of time. I had returned to the area with tens of thousands of dollars' worth of damages to two houses. The buyers of the older house wanted everything repaired and brought back to the original condition before they would purchase it. The contractor of the new house had evacuated and had not returned. Many workers were displaced. Many houses were damaged and needing repairs. The cost of materials skyrocketed. So much turmoil again!

Thankfully, I had insurance which covered some of the damages, but the cost of repairs was more than the insurance allowed. So many houses needed repairs but so few workers were available. Repairs were made to the older house while we waited for the repairs to be done on the new construction. Floors were redone. Downed trees had to be removed off the new house and off the land. Roofs and water damaged wood had to be replaced. As a single mother, all of this was totally overwhelming. I was that rubber band that was stretched to the "max."

The day came when the buyers of our old house wanted to sign papers. They needed a house too. We were no where near ready to move into our new house due to the hurricane. The construction had been delayed with a lack of workers and many repairs needing to be done before the construction could be continued. Fortunately, a friend came to our rescue and brought a camper to our property for my children and me to live in while our house was being completed. Many people were living in campers because of damaged homes. I would work all day, go to the Laundromat to wash and dry clothes, dump sewage at night, and work in the new house when I could. I was emotionally and physically exhausted. I was too weak at that point in my life when he started calling me again.

My ex-husband had contacted my kids when we had evacuated to make sure that we were safe. My oldest son had a cell phone that his dad could call anytime, but he had rarely called them. He had even gone back to the evacuated areas to check on our houses after the hurricane and had called a report back. He did not have my cell phone number since it was changed with the death threat, so he could not call me. He started calling my children more and more. He beeped me one day on my work beeper and not thinking, I called him back. Unfortunately, he then had my phone number. He started calling me. I had made a huge mistake by even listening to him. He told me how sorry he was that he had hurt me. He told me how much he missed me and wanted me back. He told me that he had had several girlfriends but broke up with them since he still loved me. He knew that I was stressed and wanted to help me and our children. He told me that he was a changed man—that he had quit drinking, quit smoking, quit cursing and had turned to God. He said that he was a true Christian now, just what I had prayed for many years.

CHAPTER 19

Reopening Doors

"The key of the house of David I will lay on His shoulder; So He shall open, and no one shall shut; And He shall shut, and no one shall open."
Isaiah 22:22(NKJV)

Again, it seems that it would be easy to avoid someone that has abused you and hurt you repeatedly for years. However, it is not easy when those soul-ties remain attached. When people want so much to believe that someone has changed, it becomes easy for them to be manipulated again. They see the good and unfortunately, ignore the bad things despite knowing that they were tricked before. Many abused women have been accused of "wanting it" or "asking for it" when they are attacked again. Many people don't understand why a victim begins to trust their abuser again. It's like the victim gives their abuser a second, third, fourth, or more chances to hurt them again. Actually, it's just that the victim may give them a second, third, or fourth chance to really change. Those words—"I have changed"— are like a magic magnet that immediately draws a person in again. That is all that the victim has wanted to restore their family—he/she wants the abuser to change. When someone loves another so deeply, it is very easy to forgive that person and believe them, despite being hurt by him/her. Those soul ties keep pulling the victim into that door or relationship if just a small crack in the door becomes opened. The best thing for the victim, especially if she is emotionally weak, is to keep that relationship closed. Also, keep praying. Seek the Lord for the healing and deliverance that can only come from Him.

This is where my story continues again…

I made a huge mistake by answering his first phone call. That put a crack in the door that had been closed by the legal system when he threatened to kill me. I actually felt sorry for him because he had not seen the kids in months, and I knew that he was concerned since the hurricanes. One call turned to several. His sister visited me and told me that he had really changed. She told me that he no longer drank, smoke, or cursed. She told me that he read his Bible, went to church, and had really turned to God. They both said the things that I had told them needed to happen for us to get back together. They both reminded me that I had said that he could date me after we divorced if he truly loved me and had changed. They were both now saying that he loved me. She and her husband had gotten back together. She wanted me and her brother to get back together. He had started offering to help me. The kids started going to his house, and the laundry was done there. He started helping me with the new house. He actually asked me to remarry him. I told him that the children and I needed to trust him more. I told him that trust had to be earned. I told the children that he had asked me to remarry him. They all said that they did not want him back in the house. My own children did not want their own father back in the house with us. My oldest threatened to move out if I ever let his father back in the house. They still did not trust him.

Several months passed during this time. He had asked me several times to marry him, but I had refused. I kept telling him that we needed more time to trust him again. None of us totally trusted him. There were so many wounds in all of us from his past behaviors. I had seen how he could pretend to change for a time; then the real personality would show itself again. The children would visit him and come back home to tell me that he had my pictures all over his house. The Protective Order had reverted to a Permanent Injunction sometime during this period after the hurricanes. My son was still afraid of his uncle and did not want to have any contact with him. The restraining order protected me and my children from any harassment from my ex and his family.

For over a year, I had had a nightmare about my ex trying to kill me. I kept having the same recurring nightmare even after the kids and I had moved into our new house. In my dream, I walked out of my bedroom into the living area. I looked out of the French doors to see my ex-husband standing in the dark on the patio with a gun pointed at me to kill me. During the construction of the house, several changes were made from the original blueprints. One night, in the dark, I woke up and walked into my living room from my bedroom after having that nightmare. At that moment, I realized that I was standing in the exact spot that I was in the recurrent dream that I had been having for over a year. I looked out the French doors into the dark. The changes that the builder had made matched the vision that I saw in my dream. I knew at that point that this dream had been a warning. One day, my ex-husband admitted that he was so angry that he had really wanted me dead. He told me that if he could have gotten his hands on me, he would have killed me. He never told anyone the truth. He had always denied it until that day. That was the end of that recurrent nightmare. However, the fear of someone watching me from the patio remained. I kept feeling that someone was watching me from those very same doors.

CHAPTER 20

The Other Woman

"Deliver my soul, O Lord, from lying lips and from a deceitful tongue."
Psalm 120:2 (NKJV)

Many abused women have such strong soul ties to their abuser that they just keep falling into that trap of manipulation and lies. The moment that they start to trust again or believe the lies is when the person with the abusive personality has control again. It is very difficult for a trusting, truthful person to continuously watch for signs of deceit. It is not in his/her nature, and he/she may repeatedly fall back into the pattern of being naive and trusting. Consequently, victims continuously miss warning signs that something is being hidden from them.

The best thing again for a victim of abuse when detachment is obtained is to remain detached. Stay away from the person who has abused you. A person can pretend to change for a long period of time just like in the initial stages of romance when someone is on their best behavior. Only time will tell if they have really changed or not. Also, keep praying. God is the only One who knows everyone's true heart. He is really also the only

One who can break those emotional ties so that the victim can get on with his/her life and the healing can begin.

This is where my story continues again…

One weekend, the children came home telling me that their dad said that he still loved me and had my pictures all over his house. The next time they went, a few weeks later, they told me that all of my pictures were gone, and he had pictures of another woman all over his house. He had not changed. He had lied and manipulated me again while he had another woman in his life. When we talked, he informed me that they were engaged to be married. He had gone from begging me to remarry him (even wanting to give me a new engagement ring) to being engaged in just a few short months. I found out that she worked with him at a school for several months. I also found out that while he was asking me to marry him, he was dating her on the side. I had been tricked and manipulated again. I had fallen for his lies again. The kids had not wanted him in our house again because they did not trust him. He told me all about his fiancé. He said that they would be getting married in a few months. He told me that she had been married twice to the same man and it didn't work out. He said that he did not want the same thing happening to us. I reminded him that the kids and I had needed to trust him and obviously we were correct. He said that he wanted me to meet her one day. He also said that he knew that I would love her. Then, I will always remember the following words that he said to me—

"She is just like you—SWEET, KIND, INNOCENT, AND NAIVE!"

I knew at that point that he had found a new person that he could abuse and manipulate. He had found another me! He had found someone who had not seen the truth yet. I started praying for her. I also continued praying for myself. I had allowed that old wound to be opened wide open again. I had allowed him back into my life to hurt me again. I was starting to trust him. I thanked God that my kids were still smart enough to see through him. His sister told me that it was entirely my fault. She told me he wanted to marry me, but that I could not expect to keep a man waiting forever. I was being blamed again. I realized that he just wanted what I could give him—his children, a new house, an extra income. He had been lying to me again. And, now he had this poor other woman who was just like me, according to him, that he could use and abuse just like he did to me.

I had been emotionally beat down again. How could I let that man hurt me again? How could I begin to trust him again? How could I be so stupid? I prayed more and more for God to help me. I kept praying for Him to reveal Himself to me. I kept crying and crying and crying out to the Lord. I had managed to become emotionally devastated again. I kept praying for God to heal me. I kept praying for God to deliver me from the bondage that I was under and that all of those soul-ties would be forever broken.

After several days of almost nonstop crying and praying, my Savior, my Healer, my Deliverer, my Lord Jesus Christ revealed Himself to me in a way that I never expected and will never forget. I was alone at my house. I had walked out onto the patio where I was still crying and praying. No one was there but me. I got up from the patio swing and walked toward the door to go back into my house. I suddenly had a strange feeling that started on the top of my head. It was like a rolling wave of total peace—an indescribable Peace—that started on the top of my head and transcended slowly down to the bottom of my feet. In this feeling of almost floating and total peace like being in another dimension or another spiritual realm, I heard His Voice behind me. In a voice from about six feet behind me where I had just been sitting, I heard clearly and loudly in an audible voice as my Lord, JESUS CHRIST called my first name and said,

"<u>EVERYTHING IS GOING TO BE OK!</u>"

CHAPTER 21

Spiritual Abuse

"Even so, every good tree bears good fruit, but a bad tree bears bad fruit."
Matthew 7:17 (NKJV)

When an abusive person claims to have changed and turned to God, the abuse takes on a different form if they have not truly changed. Instead of physical and verbal abuse with yelling and screaming, the abuse takes another dimension of abuse—a form of a "holier than thou" attitude. It changes to a different undertone which still involves an emotional abuse. The person may begin to claim that they are better than others spiritually. The abuser also claims that they may be more perfect now. They may brag about what God has told them or done for them. They may want to "lay hands and pray for you" so that you can be brought up to the new spiritual level with them. All of these things are warning signs for a known abuser, especially when these comments are accompanied by an uneasy feeling. The presence of God is peaceful. When someone is tearing you down emotionally while talking about how great he/she is spiritually, it should be a big neon warning sign.

The Word of God talks about trees and fruit. A good tree produces good fruit. A bad tree produces bad fruit. A person is known by the fruit that they produce, and a "good tree" does not produce bad fruit. This means that a "good" person does not exhibit "bad" behaviors—lying, cheating, manipulating, intimidating, scheming, anger, frustration, resentment, lust, etc. This is very important in discerning any person. Every person should evaluate what kind of fruit they produce themselves— whether good or bad.

This is where my story continues…

I was being emotionally abused in an entirely new form. Every time he called me, I was getting more and more upset. He was telling me how much he had changed. He was telling me that I had missed out on getting exactly what I had been praying for. He was telling me that he was now the Godly man that I had wanted him to be all of those years. He actually told me that I was "not Christian enough" for him now. He was telling me that he had quit smoking and quit drinking. He was telling me that he had quit cursing and had turned totally to the Lord. He was telling me that he was Spirit-filled and that I wasn't. I knew what God had done for me, filling me with His total peace and presence, but I could not tell my ex this. His words were tearing me down again. He told me that he wanted to lay hands on me and pray for me to come up to his level spiritually. I was feeling so shameful. I was feeling so guilty. Surely I must be doing something wrong. I kept repenting for any sins that I had possibly committed. I kept praying for forgiveness and for me to forgive everyone that had hurt me. I was told by him that the chances of me finding a new husband at my age would be slim. He repeatedly told me that I had lost my chances with him. He had found a new Christian woman to be his wife. He was saying that he was changed, but I was feeling horrible. My children and I had been attending a Spirit-filled Church. I had been praying for him to change. Why now? Was I envious? Why was he upsetting me? I was in an emotional turmoil again.

After the hurricanes, I had attended a conference on abuse with a close friend. This Spirit-filled Christian counselor was a "Trauma Specialist." With the encouragement of this friend, I started bringing my children to this Christian counselor. As my children and I would tell her about the events in our lives from the last several years, she acknowledged the abuse and helped us work through it. She also said that I had PTSD from all the events of the past. Any seemingly small thing would trigger severe anxiety and fear. When this new abuse started, she was already aware of what had been happening and immediately recognized the spiritual abuse that was now taking place. My children still did not want him to attend their counseling sessions. He would still get angry. The children and I were still blamed for everything. All of the counselors that we had seen had told me that the best thing that I could do was to move my children away from the area. They all knew that my children and I feared him and his outbursts and violence. That fear had never resolved.

My children would talk to him some days on the phone or see him for a day or so but avoided long periods with him. They had actually developed a system at some point between themselves to help each other to even minimize their time on the phone with him and avoid him. There was one day that my youngest son was on the phone with his dad. His sister started telling him loudly to hurry because she needed to call a friend. He hurriedly got off the phone with his dad, telling him that she needed the phone. I proceeded to hand my daughter the phone when they both, simultaneously, told me that she did not need to use it. I looked at both of them in bewilderment. It was only then that they informed me that they had been using some kind of signals to each other to help and protect each other. They would never tell me their system. In fact, they made me leave the room when they told their counselor their secret which has still never been revealed. They still help each other to get off the phone with him or totally avoid him when they sense his anger. We had all gone into a protective mode.

I had moved across town to a new subdivision, but I was not feeling any safer. My children did not want to move away from the area. I was still in an emotional whirlwind, not fully understanding that there was really a spiritual world with battles of good versus evil. I knew that God loved me. I knew that I had felt His Indescribable Presence. I knew that I had felt a total peace that was not of this earthly world. It was a peace where nothing else mattered. I knew that most people did not believe that God spoke audibly to people today—but He had spoken audibly to me. My Lord had told me, "Everything is going to be OK". It was so sacred that I had only told my sister and children. So, if everything is going to be ok, why did everything feel so wrong? As an immature Christian, I still did not have the understanding or discernment to decipher what was happening. Every time that I spoke to my ex husband, he was making me feel more and more unworthy of God's love. But, I knew that God had told me that everything was going to be ok. I prayed and prayed for help and guidance.

One morning, my phone rang very early while the children still slept. It would have been our 24th wedding anniversary. My ex-husband proceeded to tell me how he wanted to help me get to a new level spiritually like he was. He wanted to lay hands on me and pray for me. He was telling me how to speak in tongues. He was going on and on about his relationship with God. I was getting in an emotional knot. Something was wrong. I knew that the Peace of the Lord was not there. The thought came to me that I needed to stop talking to him—forever.

I told him during that phone call that it was great that he was seeking the Lord, and it was great that he had changed. I told him that I was happy for him that he had found someone and was getting married. However, I told him that he did not need to lay hands on me and pray for me. I had my own family and church family that prayed for me. I told him that he could contact the children, but I felt that it was best if he did not call me again. I did not want to talk to him again. I needed time to heal.

CHAPTER 22

Healing Begins

*"To all who mourn in Israel, He will give a crown of beauty for ashes,
a joyous blessing instead of mourning, festive praise instead of despair.
In their righteousness, they will be like great oaks that the
LORD has planted for His own glory."*
Isaiah 61:3 (NLT)

When a person has a wound, as long as they keep picking on it or pulling off the scab, the wound will not heal. The wound will stay wide open. This is what happens when a victim of abuse continues to communicate with their abuser. The wounds of abuse will not heal because they are constantly getting re-infected with some type of dirt—whether verbal, emotional, physical, spiritual or financial "dirt" or abuse. It takes time away from re-infection for the healing to occur. God can always do a miraculous healing if He chooses, but often times He allows the healing to come in stages. These stages of healing are like peeling an onion—layer by layer. These wounds after years of abuse are very deep and may take years to heal. The whole mindset has to be changed. People have to relearn who they really are. They also have to learn who they are in Christ and have to be delivered from all the afflictions of the past. The soul ties and generational ties have to be broken for a new person to emerge from the ashes.

However, an abuser has always had control over his victim. As the victim tries to regain control of his/her own life, the potential for anger and violence continues to increase. Unless the abuser has been totally delivered from his own abusive behavior traits, those abusive tendencies will continue to be exposed or revealed, despite claiming that he has changed.

Again, this is where my story continues…

I knew with that phone call that something was wrong. I recognized a turmoil that kept brewing inside of me. I knew that God loved me. He had told my sister when my ex-husband had come to kill me. He had saved me. I knew that He had filled me with His Presence. I had felt the Peace of the Lord, and this was not it. I knew that I had to stop talking to this man that had hurt me so much. But I had so many questions.

He continued to keep calling my house, usually when the children were still sleeping. I told him to call only in the evenings when the kids were home from school and awake. Many times I would not even answer the phone. I wanted to break all contact with him if possible. I told him that we could communicate about the children by email. The children kept telling me that he was angry and fussing on the phone with them. I still feared his anger but thought that it was my problem now. He emailed me one day that he was going to disown the children because they did not want to see him or spend much time with him. His anger or "fruit" was still revealing itself, but everyone kept saying that he was a changed man, a new Christian.

I kept praying for God to help me to understand. I kept crying out to Him and asking Him why. I had been told that the chances of me getting another husband were slim at my age, but I had told my ex that God was big enough to bring a husband to my door when He was ready. I had faith that God could do anything. I knew that God could heal my fear and totally deliver him from his anger. But, I asked God why He didn't change my husband years before as I had prayed. I repeatedly asked the Lord why He was changing him now — for another woman. I had never looked at another man. I still was not looking for another man. I would have waited for him to change. I would have waited for our family to be restored.

These same questions were repeatedly asked as I cried and cried for days again. I was feeling so hurt again. I could not understand why God was changing him now. Why was he a Godly man now when I needed him to change years before for me and our children? I cried out to the Lord and asked for forgiveness. I prayed for total healing and deliverance. I continuously cried out to the Lord to help me through all of this.

One day, I was walking around our block. My children were tired of seeing me cry, so I was walking around the block as I prayed and cried. I kept asking God the same questions again and again. I kept asking for forgiveness and felt that maybe I had not forgiven him and his family enough for me to be blessed. I could not understand why God had started changing him now after all of those years of praying for him to change. I prayed that God would help me and my children to forgive him and his family for hurting us so much. I prayed for everyone who had hurt us and that God would forgive them. I kept praying for help, for guidance, for forgiveness, for deliverance, for healing—for everything that I could even possibly think of. After walking and praying and crying for about an hour, I went back home.

As soon as I walked into my house, my phone rang. I picked it up to hear:

HE IS A LIAR!
HE IS A DECIEVER!
HE IS A MANIPULATOR!
HE IS AN ABUSER!
HE IS A MURDERER!
HE WANTED YOU DEAD!
THE ONLY REASON YOU ARE NOT DEAD IS BECAUSE
 YOUR DAUGHTER WAS WITH YOU!
HE HAS NOT CHANGED!
HE WILL NEVER CHANGE!
HE WOULD HAVE HURT YOU AGAIN!
HE WILL HURT THIS OTHER WOMAN!
HE WILL NEVER CHANGE!!!

I stood in my house in total shock. It was a quick call, no introduction, no other chit-chat. I had received a message and that was it. I was crying. The call had been so quick. I picked up an ink pen and pad of paper. I redialed the home number and told the caller that I was ready to write the message down. This person lived hours away in another part of the state and could not have known that I had just been walking and praying and crying to the Lord for answers. I asked the person to restate what was just told to me. The response shocked me even more…

I said, "Please repeat what you just told me so I can write it down."

I heard, "What?
I said, "You just called me!"
I heard, "I did?"
I said, "Yes! You just called me! Please repeat what you told
 me!"
I heard, "I can't."

I said, "Why can't you? You just called me!"

I heard, "I don't know what was said."

I said, "How can you not know what you just said?"

I heard, "It was not me."

I said, "Yes, it was you! You called me!"

I heard, "I may have called you, but it was not me—it was the
    Holy Spirit giving you a message directly."

I repeated, "How can you not know?"

I heard, "The Holy Spirit uses people to speak to other people.
    If it was not meant for me then it would not go to my head
    where I would remember it. It only went from my heart and
    out of my mouth."

I said, "I don't understand. How can that be?"

I heard, "God uses people as vessels to deliver His message. I
    was just His vessel."

I told the caller that I had just been walking, praying, and talking to God and this was exactly the answers that I had been desperately seeking from God. Only God knew this!!

God answered all of those questions that I had been crying and praying about. He knows everyone's heart! God had just told me that my ex had not really changed. He told me what was really on his heart. In the New Testament, it says that if you have hate in your heart, then you are a murderer in God's eyes. God revealed the truth to me instead of the lies that I was hearing.

Then, God revealed to me more about how He uses people to give messages. The Lord showed me that these Godly people, who had stood by my side and said these same things to me about my ex, were really relaying His message the entire time. I had failed to listen to them, thinking that it was their own personal opinions. It took this phone call (where this person did not really remember calling and did not even know what was said) to open my eyes to the "Truth" and the possibilities of the spiritual realm when a person totally gives his/her life to God. There is nothing impossible with God!

The Word of God says, "The Truth shall set you free." (John 8:32) I had received the Truth!!! I had been torn between what I was hearing here on earth from people who can be deceived and what I had continued to see and hear with "bad fruit" or anger coming from him. I had wanted him to change so much for me and our children and had been deceived again by his words, despite his actions. I knew that God was never deceived. I felt a new freedom that I had not felt before. I felt so loved by God. He had reached out to me again in my state of brokenness. I felt that more bondages of the past were breaking off of me. I could now let go of the hope that my ex-husband would someday change, because God knows all—today, tomorrow, and forever.

I knew now that I could never trust him and that he would never change. I had heard it directly from God Himself. I knew that I had a lot of healing that needed to be done with the deep-rooted fear that had been embedded within me, but the healing had really begun that day. I knew that God was healing me, delivering, and revealing His love for me. I began praying that I would one day be a pure vessel that God could use to relay His pure messages, just like I had received that day, to the broken and injured people of this world to truly begin their path to healing and that all of us abused people would have a crown of beauty for the ashes of our past.

CHAPTER 23

Financial Abuse

"There was a certain rich man who had a steward, and an accusation was brought to him that this man was wasting his goods."
Luke 16:1-3(NKJV)

There are so many names of types of abuse: emotional abuse, verbal abuse, physical abuse, psychological abuse, sexual abuse, spiritual abuse, child abuse, elder abuse, and even financial abuse. Anything that is used to hurt someone can be considered an abuse. When someone intentionally does not work to support a family, it is a financial abuse. When someone spends all the money on his own wants and desires, it is also a financial abuse. The Bible talks about being "good stewards" of what God gives each person. This means using it wisely and helping others in need. Any intentional wasting or destructive action meant to use someone or cause some type of injury to a person or their well-being can be considered an abusive treatment of people or resources.

When a person is being recurrently abused, many times they don't even recognize it. They are so "brainwashed" or so used to things being a certain way that it appears normal to them. There are so many examples: The child slapped in the face by an angry parent; The bedridden elderly hit by a caretaker; The woman verbally abused by a husband; The lonely teenager bullied at school; The child touched inappropriately by an adult; The elderly person, whose savings gets emptied out by "family" instead of the money being used for their care; The victims who get death threats. These are all various abuses that occur daily. Some victims are too young or old and scared to report anything. Most victims of recurrent abuses accept things as a normal part of their life. They tolerate some of these abuses. The innocent victim may have to have someone discover the abuse and fight for him/her. The other victims have to be willing to be receptive and believe when family or friends that care for them express concerns for an abusive action that keeps recurring. Sometimes, someone may need to step up and call it what it is—abuse.

This is where my story continues on this subject…

Again, most of the time, I had no idea that I was even being abused. My children and I lived in it and tolerated it as normal behavior. Many people came to me after the separation and divorce to express concerns for what they had witnessed for years. Amazingly to me, two other couples who were our closest friends during different stages of our lives, came to me and stated the same things that our oldest friends had told me the day of his death threat. These three couples did not know each other, but all three reported the same things. They had all spent a lot of time with us and watched as his abusive ways became increasingly obvious. He exhibited more and more abuse to me and the children in front of these friends as time progressed. It was like he would let his guard down in front of them. They all reported that they could not stand to watch his abuse anymore and that it was obvious that I did not even realize what he was doing to me and the children. All of these couples—one from the beginning of our marriage to our first child, one from our first through second child, then one from the time when my ex went to work for the police department right after the birth of our last child—were all reporting the same things about how abusive he was to me during each of those three different stages of our marriage. They all told me that they could not stand to watch the abuse any longer and started making excuses to avoid us. These couples did not even know each other! I told each of them that he had repeatedly told me that I was mean, controlling, and abusive to him. They all adamantly denied that, telling me that I was always trying to please him, but he was always mean to me—to my face and behind my back. It was really only after we split up that the word "abuse" even surfaced. Some friends and some coworkers had witnessed it and told me to stand up to him when he repeatedly called me and yelled at me. Some of his own coworkers came forward in support of me and told me about some of his irrational behaviors at work and mean things that he had said about me for years. Many people came forward and told me how he had repeatedly abused me and used me for many years. I had believed his lies and blamed myself for years, but now more and more people were reporting being witnesses to his abuses. Amazingly, I had heard all the terms of the different abuses—except one.

I had repeatedly been asked why I "allowed" him to buy so many new vehicles. I was asked many times why I "allowed" him to buy so many new campers, guns, boats, etc. Many people asked me why I let him quit work to go to school. I was even asked by my own parents why I always wanted new things and was never satisfied. He had even manipulated my own parents by telling them that I was asking for the new things. I could never stop him! He would be angry until he got what he wanted, no matter what the cost. His previous coworkers told me what he had said for years when he was questioned about his repeated purchases. He always said, "My wife is a nurse. I don't even have to work," or "I can afford it; I can buy whatever I want." I had always believed that one day I could afford to stop working full time to be home more with our children, but our bank account would never increase to that point. Everything that would have a cash value would eventually be cashed in or used up to purchase a "new toy." He was always buying and trading. Even his own family had laughed about him always getting new vehicles. I never had a name for it or understood it.

There was a day when my middle child and I were in our new house. We were quietly watching TV and had placed the channel on some Christian network. As soon as we started listening to this unknown pastor or minister, he spoke and pointed his finger toward us, and his words hit me like a lightening bolt. He said,

"There are some of you women out there who have been abused—emotionally abused, verbally abused, physically abused, sexually abused, spiritually abused, and yes, even **financially abused...**"

When those words, "financially abused," were spoken, I went into an uncontrollable shaking. My entire body including my whole jaw was not just shivering; it was shaking uncontrollably, or the word "quaking" is more of an accurate description. I could not even speak. I had absolutely no control of my body, especially my jaw as it repeatedly slammed together. I burst into a fit of tears as he continued speaking. He said,

"God does not want you to be abused any longer!"

I knew that God was talking to me directly. I could not speak as I tried to contact my sister to tell her what was happening to me. The Holy Spirit had just touched me and had complete control of my body. I could not talk with my jaw jumping uncontrollably. My son got on the phone and explained to my sister what was happening to me. I knew that God had just revealed something to me that I knew nothing about—financial abuse.

More and more thoughts flooded my mind. My ex had always told me that my family was some of the wealthiest in the area (which was not accurate). He had grown up in a very poor family with the bare minimum. His mother made some of his clothes out of sack cloths as a child. They had to scrape by month after month to put food on the table. My family had a lot more. However, they were not wealthy. They had something that his family didn't—some money in savings. I realized that I was his "gold mine." I knew that some abusers withheld money to keep their spouses at home under their control. However, I did not realize that it was also financial abuse to use a family for their resources or to take advantage of a spouse by intentionally not working to adequately support a family or intentionally over spending family finances. At that moment, I realized that I had been used again.

We had come from different worlds. I realized that he had used me and my family to get ahead financially from the first day that we were married. I had fallen in love with a poor man, despite warnings from all of my family that he could not provide for me. I never let lack of money be an issue in our relationship, knowing that we could make it if we worked together. I had put him through college to get an education at his request. I would try to save for our future, and he would constantly spend for his immediate pleasures. I had innocently watched as he spent thousands and thousands of dollars every year despite my concerns. I had never understood why he always spent so much money.

Now, I realized that he had used me and abused me financially as well. I had been his ticket to financial advancement. He had already told me that he never really loved me. He had already told me that he was told that

I was too good for him, but he showed them because he married me. He was the one that always spoke about my parents being "rich," and I would deny it because I never saw it. I knew that they had some savings, but the definition of comfortable versus rich versus wealthy depends on each person's view point. He had been looking up from the bottom of the "glass" where he grew up in poverty. I was looking at the middle of the glass from a view point of a middle class person, knowing the importance of saving for the future. I realized that he had manipulated his way out of poverty.

Again, I felt that my entire life had been a lie. I never knew why he had always spent and spent and spent our money till God revealed it to me. I never even realized that there was a term for it till that day—financial abuse.

CHAPTER 24

Truth

"And you shall know the truth, and the truth shall set you free."
John 8:32 (NKJV)

The walking wounded, the abused people of this world, have so many wounds from the past. When more abuse is exposed, it opens up the old wounds that are already so deep. Once the wounds are opened, healing can occur from deep within.

A major part of the healing process is the revelation of the truth. When the truth is revealed, it may hurt initially (and may hurt a lot), but once the truth is exposed, the lie can no longer hurt you. The person then has a chance to deal with the truth and the pain that accompanies it. Some people feel that withholding the truth or keeping a "little white lie" won't hurt someone or may protect them in some cases. However, when that lie, deceit, or manipulation is exposed, it can be very hurtful and harmful. It not only hurts to know that you have been lied to, but it can be a destructive force that destroys the foundation of trust that some relationships are built on.

The Word says, "The truth shall set you free." Yes, the truth shall set you free—physically, emotionally and spiritually. Once the truth is exposed, you are no longer held bondage to the lies that you were told. The wounds formed by lies can then begin to heal once the truth is revealed. This healing takes time as layer upon layer of wounds are opened. There is also an old saying, "Time heals all wounds." This is because most healing comes in stages in time, but God can do a miraculous healing.

This is where my story continues again…

I started crying out to the Lord within months of my marriage to my abusive husband. However, when my husband was being nice, I wanted my husband—not God. When my husband was mean, I wanted God back in my life. I was like a constant yo-yo in my walk with God. It was only when I was consistently hitting "rock bottom" that I truly, wholly gave my heart to God and started seeking Him every day. It was at that point that God started revealing Himself to me, but I did not even realize it. I kept praying, but God does not always answer prayers the way that we want them—because he knows everyone's heart.

I have already written about some of the things that God did for me through all of my trials and tribulations up to this point. When God revealed the financial abuse to me, I realized that He had revealed another truth to me that had been hidden deep within my ex-husband's heart. I had never heard of this kind of "financial abuse," but it definitely explained what I had lived with for all of those years of working and struggling to try to save some money for our future. It released me from the hurt and wounds from all those years that I heard that I was selfish, controlling, and mean when I would try to reason with him about his frequent major purchases.

I started praying for the whole truth to be revealed. I constantly prayed that everything that had been done in the darkness to be brought to the light. I knew that a key to my healing was in the revelation of the truth.

Early one morning, I woke up at 3:44. I suddenly realized that I had been waking up at that same time almost daily for probably over a year. I realized that is was impossible without an alarm clock. I sat up suddenly when I realized it and grabbed my Bible. I knew that God was communicating with me. The Book of Psalms came to my mind so I looked up the verses that corresponded to the time—Psalm 3 and Psalm 44 for 3:44 am. The following verses are where I felt God touching me and revealing something to me:

> *"I lay down and slept;*
> *I woke up in safety,*
> *For the Lord was watching over me."*
> *Psalm 3:5(NLT)*
> *"It is You who gives us victory over our enemies;*
> *It is You who humbles those who hate us."*
> *Psalm 44:7(NLT)*

I felt that God was telling me to trust and have faith in Him and He would take care of me. Also, I realized that the Lord was telling me that He had been protecting me. I had already had several death threats and multiple dreams of my ex standing on my patio in the dark to kill me. God had been protecting me while I slept during all of that time. It actually gave me a new meaning to the old saying, "Time heals all wounds." God was using the clock to reveal truths and bring healing to me.

I had already stopped phone contact with my ex-husband at this point, but only after I felt God telling me to stop talking to him. The children would talk to him and then get off of the phone all upset because of his continued verbal abuse. He was constantly criticizing me and fussing to our children. He would tell lies about me. And, money was a major subject to fuss about. He had purchased multiple vehicles, four-wheelers, etc. since we had split up, but he no longer had my income to support his spending habits. One day, I accidentally answered the phone to hear him fussing and cussing at me. He was blaming me for the children not wanting to go see him. I reminded him that his relationship with the children was his responsibility. I also reminded him that I had a permanent restraining order that prevented him from harassing me. I kept telling him to only call at night when the children were home. He could email me about the children (that way it was written proof), but he had to be nice.

Well, initially, the emails were nice communication about when the children would go see him and about God; then, the anger started showing and could be felt as I read the emails. I was still getting abused even through the internet. He would fuss about money, the children not wanting to go to see him, the children not calling him enough, etc.

One day, I got very upset with him and responded in a long email to all of his accusations that had been accumulating. I told him in the email all of the reasons that the children did not want to be near him. I gave him many examples of his behavior. I was upset that this man could even harass me by email. As I tried to "send" my response, my email would not send. I tried and tried multiple times. Other emails were sent but this one would not leave my computer. I saved it as a draft to send at a later time.

The next morning, I woke up at 4:04. Immediately, I felt that the Lord was telling me something. I sat up and turned on the light. Again, I felt that the Lord was telling me The Book of Psalms again. I opened my Bible to read Psalm 4:4. Imagine my surprise when I read...

> *"Don't sin by letting anger gain control over you.*
> *Think about it overnight and remain silent."*
> *(Psalm 4:4, NLT)*

Oh, my God. You were telling me that it was ok to be upset with him but not to sin by lashing back at him in anger—just be still and silent. I knew that God was telling me that He knew what was happening and for me to just rest in Him. Needless to say, that email draft was deleted when I got to work that day instead of sending it to my ex-husband.

I knew that God was helping me and teaching me. I just kept praying for more truths to be revealed. I felt that when I knew the truth, the doors for healing were opened. I had so much pain and so many questions—how could I have been so blind. I kept asking The Lord, "Why?"

Then one morning, I woke up at 4:19. I sat straight up in bed. I felt God's presence. I also heard "Genesis," I turned to Genesis, but this time I knew that it was two different chapters again, 4 and 19.

Genesis 4 is the story about Cain and Abel. The Lord asks Cain, "Why are you so angry?" Cain was filled with so much anger and resentment toward his brother that he killed him. Cain murdered his own brother, Abel.

Genesis 19 is the story about Lot and his family being saved before Sodom and Gomorrah were destroyed. There was so much corruption in that area that God was planning to destroy it. However, Lot was the only righteous person left. God sent His angels as men who grabbed the hands of Lot, his wife, and two daughters and rushed them to safety before the cities were destroyed by God. However, Lot's wife looked back despite warnings not to look back and turned to a pillar of salt.

Then, as I lay in my bed, awake after reading these two chapters at 4:19 in the morning, I had my first vision. It was like watching a movie. I saw my ex-husband and me with his back to me. I was crying hysterically and repeatedly asking him, "Why?? What did I do? What happened? Why? Tell me why!" After minutes of this crying out and begging him for answers, I watched as he slowly turned to me. He then slowly said like he was surprised, "You really did love me!" The vision ended at that time, but I kept asking the Lord to show me more.

I had realized in that moment that God was telling me that my exhusband was so full of anger like Cain that he was capable of murder. And, just like righteous Lot and his family, God had moved me and my children away to a new location. I also realized that my ex was so full of anger and resentment, that he did not even realize what he actually had, until he lost it all. He was just like Cain.

God had showed me the truth and had helped me to see that it was not me. I had lived around corruption for years and had tried to maintain truthfulness and righteousness, always trying to teach my children right instead of wrong. I had been accused for years of being mean, hateful, controlling, manipulative, etc— I had been blamed for everything! I had apologized a million times for things that I had not even done just to make peace. But God knew the truth. He had just told me that he rescued me like Lot.

The saying "Time heals all wounds" is so significant, but this was a different way. God was using the clock and time to communicate with me and reveal the truths to me that I had not accepted from family and friends. Well, the time "4:19" brought a tremendous amount of healing to me. God had showed me that it was not my fault through those scriptures and that vision. I had been told that many times by people who loved me.

However, in that moment coming from God (who does not lie), I knew that I was truly innocent. I just sat in bed and cried as years of pain and wounds were being healed in that moment.

God continued to wake me up many mornings with messages from Him with the time on the clock. He has told me how much He loves me, how He is protecting me, what is happening in some situations, and has even directly answered many questions that I have asked Him to reveal the answer. Many people would say that someone is crazy for believing that, but over the years, God has continued to speak to me through time on the clock, through numbers, through songs, and many other ways. Sometimes, we just need to open our hearts to Him so that we can hear that "Small, still voice."

CHAPTER 25

More Truths

"To give light to those who sit in darkness and the shadow of death,
to guide our feet into the way of peace."
Luke 1:79(NKJV)

Whenever someone is a victim in an abusive relationship, their lives are surrounded by outbursts of anger, bitterness, resentment, frustration, etc. which causes fear, confusion, and an uncertainty to increase with each attack. It is these intimidation tactics that are used to control a victim. All of these negative feelings in an abusive personality seems to build up like a kettle of boiling water until it "blows off steam" causing that abusive person to lash out at the person with the least resistance—those who are innocent or already victimized who have become passive. These abusive characteristics can be disguised from an authoritarian position such as a parent, a teacher, a police officer, a boss, etc. However, the abuser still uses the same tactics—harassment, intimidation, threats, isolation, yelling, etc. on every victim, whether young or old.

This is where my story continues again....

I kept praying for more and more truths to be exposed. I continued to pray that all things that were done in the darkness to be brought to the light. I knew that God was the only One who knew all truths and was bringing healing to my mind, soul, and spirit. I knew that he had revealed the anger that still existed in my ex-husband despite the claims of being a new man, a new Christian.

My children would occasionally visit him, and many times they would come back home in tears. Despite his claims to have changed, he was very verbally abusive to our children, especially our daughter. They reported his anger to me and their counselor. They could sense it even on the phone and would try to avoid him at those times. They would come home and tell me what had happened. They still reported drinking and smoking, but it was now being done in secret. He would tell them not to say anything, especially to his "soon to be new wife". He would be drinking when he picked them up. Then he would put gloves on to light up a cigarette and smoke. When he was finished, he threw all of the evidence out of the window. He would then use mouthwash and gum and spray cologne all over him. He would even use hand sanitizer to wash his hands to hide any smell of smoke. He was not supposed to be drinking within 48 hours of visitation with the children according to the final legal papers which gave me sole custody of our children. My children did not want me to do anything. They were afraid of his outbursts and just wanted to see their dad less and less. They just kept reporting everything to me and their counselor. They helped each other with their secretive signals and tried to protect each other from his outbursts. They could tell when his anger was building by the way he treated them at the time, so they would avoid him. He had not changed, but God had already told me that their dad would never change.

Their dad's wedding day was set for a few months after he became engaged. His new fiancé' had no idea of the deceit and manipulation that was being revealed to my children. She had known him only a few months when they became engaged. He was pretending to be a different person to her. He was claiming to have quit smoking and drinking to her. He was actually teaching them how to lie and deceive people. However, they always came home and told me the truth. My children and I would get together and pray. They would pray when their dad wanted them to go see him. They would ask God to orchestrate their paths; then something would come up and their dad would cancel his plans. We all knew that God was still protecting us.

My children did not want to go to his wedding and begged me to take them out of town when the day came. We left town to go visit my brother and his family. It was on the way there that my children were talking about the wedding and how they did not want to attend. My oldest son then told us that he was not even invited. His dad had never spoken to him about the wedding or invited him. He only knew about it from his brother and sister. We happened to stop at my ex-husband's aunt's house to visit. She called to check on us frequently, and she was the only one on his side of the family that had ever asked my children to tell her the truth. She knew that my kids and I were not lying. She knew that we had all lived under an abusive situation. She knew that her own brother, my ex's dad, was an alcoholic and very abusive. He had continued in his own father's footsteps.

I had friends that would come and visit us and would continue to reveal more truths. My ex's family members were deep into legal problems due to the drugs and things found at their home. More and more witnesses to their illegal activities had stepped up and reported what had been done. I was told that state and federal agents were investigating and questioning neighbors. I even found out that they had used us unknowingly in an insurance scam at one point by claiming that our boat motor had fallen off our boat and was lost in the river. A neighbor told me that the motor was still in their possession. The best friends that lived next to my ex-sister-in-law had stopped all contact with that family. They had seen the lies, manipulation, and illegal activities and wanted no part of that lifestyle. That best friend that I had been told to leave alone was now one of my best friends. She has stood by my children and I till this day. I kept thanking God that he had moved my children and me away from that family. However, we were not far enough.

There was so much turmoil going on around us and I just kept praying. One day, I called several international ministries just for prayer. I knew that I still needed God to deliver us. I happened to speak to a woman, not realizing that she was one of God's prophets who answered the phone. What she told me shocked me but brought more clarity to my situation and healing to my soul. She gave me this message, stating that it was from the Lord:

"You had many opportunities to leave him, but you stayed by his side. God gave him many opportunities and gave him plenty of rope, and he messed up repeatedly. He is trying, but he is not following the right god. He is smart and turns everything you say around to confuse you. You do not deserve the mean things he is saying about you. His parents treated him the same way he treats you."

This woman knew nothing of me or my situation and the turmoil that I had been experiencing in my life. I had just called a Christian ministry phone number for prayer. I knew that God was helping me to know more of the truth.

One day, a friend of mine who went to church with me and was a teacher, came to sit with me at a school function. Suddenly, she said, "I just hate your ex- husband!" I asked her why. She said that she "hated him for what he had done to me and my children and for what he does to his children in his classroom as a teacher." I was in total shock as I asked her to explain.

She stated, "I have a little girl in my class that was in his special education class at the school that he taught at previously. This little girl is terrified of men for what he did to her!" I just sat in shock, not even able to imagine what she would say. Then she continued. "She is bipolar and can be very difficult, but no one believed her because she is bipolar. This girl reported that he chased her around the classroom, yelling at her, pinching her, etc. She said he caught her and threw her out of the room into a hall where no one could see them (it was a 2 room pod with no one in the other room). She also said that he choked her with his hands around her throat against the wall and threatened to beat her while he cursed at her!" She continued to say, "This little girl is terrified of men because of this abuse!" She told me that the school moved the little girl to another school because the mother had complained, but he had denied it. She also said that "this little girl has consistently told the same story" and that she believed her. I was crying at this point and told her that the little girl was telling the truth!

I told her the whole story as I cried for this poor defenseless child...

When I was still talking to my ex, he called me one day and told me that he had had a bad day. He told me that he had chased this little bipolar girl around the classroom and had caught her and thrown her out into the hall. He then told me that he had pushed her against the wall and had choked her and had threatened to beat the sxxx out of her if she did not stop. He told me that he used pressure points that he had learned in the police academy to get control of any "out of control child."

I actually did not believe him! I had suspected that he was bipolar himself and exaggerated how upset that he was and how he had actually disciplined the children. I could not believe that he could have done that to an innocent student. He was a teacher. They were supposed to protect those children!

But, that was the key. She was an innocent special education student with mental issues that some people would not believe. He had deliberately chosen his innocent victim so that he could manipulate the entire situation in his favor.

Then I realized that there were so many things that he had told me in the past that I had never believed, just thinking that he was possibly bipolar and that he lied and exaggerated things. He once told me about getting angry at a female teacher for harassing him in class in high school. He said that in his anger, he grabbed her and held her upside down out the second story window. I never believed him. Then, years later when we were separated, our youngest son came home from his dad's house and told me that his dad had told him a story about getting mad and holding a teacher out the window by her ankles when he was a teenager. However, in that version, the teacher had no underwear on under her dress and was totally exposed. He had proudly told our son that the teacher had fallen in love with him after that incident and never harassed him again. I had told my son that the poor teacher was probably terrified of him if it had really occurred.

Things like these events were unimaginable to me. I never believed that someone could get so totally angry that they could lose all control and treat innocent people with violence. I guess in my mind, it was easier for me to believe that he was lying to me, than for me to believe that he was actually being truthful and had the potential for that kind of violence.

I knew that God was still revealing truths to me. This was a potentially violent man who was capable of hurting innocent people, even special children. He also was a liar and manipulator who managed to deceive innocent, non-suspecting people like myself and his new wife. I just continued to pray for God to protect me and my children as well as this new, innocent wife and every child that he ever came in contact with.

CHAPTER 26

Fear

"For God has not given us a spirit of fear, but of power
and of love and of a sound mind."
2 Timothy 1:7 (NKJV)

An abused person can live with PTSD (post traumatic stress disorder) similar to a soldier on a battlefield. The victim has actually been in their own battle and on their own battlefield—whether a mental, physical, or spiritual battlefield. The fear that sets in a victim is real; it is real FEAR. Just like this little girl feared men, this fear affects responses to people and future relationships due to the abuse or trauma that occurred. People that live in fear find that they are always looking over their shoulders to see if someone is following them or watching them. They tend to become suspicious of people and their motives. They tend to get anxiety attacks or panic attacks and cry easily. They actually tend to avoid people or crowds. Simple seemingly innocent things can trigger attacks. But just like a soldier may be in heightened security mode, not knowing if there is an ambush waiting around the corner in a war zone, a victim of abuse with PTSD never knows if there is an ambush of abuse waiting for them, and unknowingly, tends to live with that fear.

This is where my story continues again…

One day, my son, who was fifteen years old at the time, came home and told me that his dad had bought a new gun. I immediately broke down in an uncontrollable crying episode. Thoughts of him trying to kill me flooded my mind. It had triggered something—a fear that I had suppressed. I contacted my attorney because I did not understand what was included in this Permanent Injunction. I was contacted by the Sheriff's department after the legal papers were examined by an attorney, reportedly in the Department of Alcohol, Tobacco, and Firearms (ATF). I was told that the Protective Order that was obtained just before the hurricanes had been sent to New Orleans for his name to be added to the list of people who could never own guns again. However, when New Orleans flooded, those papers were lost. I was told that he should never purchase guns and that they would be adding his name to the list and contacting him.

When the Sheriff's Deputy called me back a few days later, he told me that he went to see my ex-husband. He said that he told him that he could never purchase guns and gave him the choice of four options:

1. Give all guns to a family member.
2. Sell the guns back to a dealer.
3. Give the guns to the police to be destroyed.
4. Be arrested.

The deputy then told me that my ex asked if he could give the guns to his son. The deputy told me that his response was that it depended on the son's age. He told me that my ex-husband told him that our son was sixteen. The deputy said that he told him that a sixteen year old was too young. He also said that he told him that if the child was eighteen years old, then he could have gotten the guns. I was informed by the deputy that my ex-husband's response was, "I have an eighteen year old son also but I am not about to give him anything! I will get rid of them first!"

I informed the sheriff's deputy that he had been lied to by my ex. My younger son had just turned fifteen years old. Our older son was eighteen years old and did not have much to do with his dad because of his behavior. The deputy informed me that my ex-husband told him that he would sell the guns back to the gun dealer. Sadly though, a large number of the guns had been purchased as gifts for our two sons over the years, but their father had them in his possession. Each son lost about five guns purchased for them over the years for birthdays and Christmases when their dad could have given them to the oldest son to hold.

The sheriff's deputy had called me back a few days later and told me that he had checked and that the guns were back with the dealer. However, my ex-husband and most police officers were good friends with the gun dealer. I never trusted that he had really gotten rid of all guns—especially when my son would come home and tell me that there were bullet casings all over his dad's backyard. My daughter also told me that there was a new gun box under her dad's bed. The children said that there were bullets all over his house and empty casings all over his backyard, but their dad would always tell them that friends came over to target practice.

I still had this fear of him wanting to kill me again if he ever got mad enough. I had seen his violence. I walked out of my house early one morning, and I found a box of fresh doughnuts sitting under my carport. I started shaking. I knew that he had been there. He had left teaching and worked shift-work at one of the local plants. I knew that he had been outside of my house as we all slept. I had installed a security system when I had built the house, but I still did not feel safe.

Another morning, I got up early and went outside to get the newspaper. Instead of me walking all the way down the driveway which was quite long, I discovered the paper right outside my back door, under my carport. I knew that he was still lurking around my house in the dark of night and early mornings. I felt like I had a stalker, but who would believe me and my fears? I just kept telling the counselors all about my concerns and fears. They believed me and always kept telling me that the best thing for me and my children was to leave the area.

Many times, my youngest son would get a phone call from his dad, telling him to come outside and meet his dad. His dad would just show up and demand that he go with him and then ride around and fuss most of the time. Once after we split up, his dad brought him some food to school before a ball game and threw it at him, hitting him in the chest, as he yelled something about never wanting to hear from anyone that he was a "bad dad" to him again. My son said that he had to struggle not to cry in front of the other boys. He was so upset that he could not even eat before the game. His dad had just verbally and emotionally abused him again.

It was this unpredictable, abusive behavior that had me and my two youngest children on edge. My daughter was still afraid of him but said that she felt safer going to his house now that he was married. He treated them nicer when his wife was around. However, they were already hearing cursing and nasty, degrading comments about his new wife when she wasn't with them. The pattern of abuse was already starting in his new marriage. Whether or not his wife knew it yet, he was already criticizing her to others to manipulate his next move or situation.

The fear that I had may seem irrational to most people, unless they have lived under the same type of death threats or abusive situations. How can a simple box of doughnuts showing up under a carport or a newspaper magically appearing outside your door under your carport trigger a state of panic or state of emergency in your mind? Why would doughnuts or a newspaper make someone cry and shake in fear? Though, it may seem innocent to most, the victim knows that the attacker was there, watching and waiting for his opportune time. It's like a serial killer leaving his "calling card" for his next intended victim. The victim knows and feels that danger is near. What if the victim would have come out of her secure place at that time? What if a door had been unlocked? What if the security system would have been off? What if the children had not been home? What if...?

In movies, when danger is coming or lurking around the corner, the music changes to a dramatic tone that puts the audience on edge, waiting for something to happen. In real life, there is no music, but there is this internal sense of danger that brings the person that has been victimized to a heightened sense of alertness. People that live with death threats like mine—"one of these days, when you least expect it...I will kill you!"—happen to live with a fear that one day their attacker will get angry and "snap" again, losing all control, and come after them again, no matter how far away, to fulfill their threat. Only the victims that have experienced the violence, the threats, and the fear know that it is REAL. However, I have come to learn that God does protect His children. He has not given us a spirit of fear; that is not from God. He has given us a sound mind and He will warn us and protect us if we turn to Him, and He will orchestrate our paths if we ask Him.

CHAPTER 27

The Miraculous

"Men of Israel, hear these words: Jesus of Nazareth, a Man attested by God to you by miracles, wonders, and signs which God did throug Him in your midst, as you yourselves also know."
Acts 2:22 (NKJV)

When someone truly reaches out to God, He is there to respond to their needs. He sees all. He hears all. He knows everyone's heart. He knows the truth. He knows ALL—everything—nothing is hidden from God.

Sometimes, people may be too upset to hear Him or not trusting Him enough to hear Him. God speaks to people in many different ways—through His own audible voice, through family, through other people, through pastors, through the Bible (His Word), through signs, through numbers, through music, and even through the clock. God speaks in innumerable ways—GOD CAN NOT BE PUT IN A BOX!!!

When we pray to God, He will begin to reveal Himself. However, God is a Gentleman and will not force Himself on anyone. He has given us the ability to choose—right or wrong, good or bad, Him or not. But, when someone really cries out to Him, He will be with them. As we continue to pray for His Revelation and His Miraculous Presence, He will draw us near to Him and show us His Mighty Hand.

This is where my story continues again…

I kept praying for God to reveal Himself more to me and my children. I kept praying that He would speak loud and clear for me to hear Him. I had been told many things over the years that had come from God, but never realized it because it came from family and friends relaying messages from Him, but I did not trust the mouth that the words were spoken out of at the time. I did not realize at the time that it was Divine Revelation.

My children and I kept praying as a family. My two youngest children had been going to a Spirit-filled church with me and were also growing closer to the Lord. We kept praying for their brother and their dad and his wife. My oldest son thought that we were crazy. His dad would let him drink, and he saw no problem with it. He did not understand that we were praying to break the cycle of alcoholism and abuse off of my children. We kept praying for God to bring us closer to Him and closer as a family. We continually prayed for Him to protect us. God had already revealed to us that He was protecting us. God had already spoken to me and told me that everything was going to be OK. I had already felt His indescribable peace. He had already told me that my ex-husband would never change, but I just kept praying.

The children were experiencing his anger, manipulation, lying, etc more and more now since I did not talk to him. There were days that all of the children avoided his calls because he was so mean to them. I did continue to see and feel his underlying abusive traits in his emails. One day he was telling me about his relationship with God and that he hoped that one day I would have what he had. Another day, he was telling me that we were going to be neighbors since his wife owned property near mine (after I had told him to stay away from me). Then, another note telling me that he hoped that the kid's counselor could help them with the guilt that they were going to feel for keeping him out of their lives. On the surface, these messages may seem innocent to some people. However, there were underlying, hidden messages in each one of these and all had a stabbing effect. We all kept feeling a turmoil that would not leave us alone. We did not realize that as we got closer to God, the spiritual battle around us was increasing, and I was in a spiritual battle for my son who did not understand yet.

I kept praying for God to guide my path. My children and I had moved to a new neighborhood across town, but there were still emotional and spiritual battles going on with their dad and his family. We were still being blamed for everything that had happened. The children were still getting emotionally and verbally abused when they did see him. I just knew that I needed God's intervention in my life to bring the peace that we so needed.

One day, as I was driving home, I was crying and praying for God to guide my path. The emotional turmoil had been so strong. Suddenly, the miraculous hand of God was revealed.

As I was driving down the road leading to my new subdivision and house, three white birds flew over my vehicle from the back. These three white birds continued to fly immediately in front of the hood of my vehicle as I drove down the road. Amazingly, these three birds turned down the road that my house was on and then turned into my driveway directly in front of my vehicle. As I turned into my driveway, the birds flew up and away into the sky.

I had just witnessed the Miraculous!

There is no way in the natural world for three white birds to do what had just happened. These birds flew that entire way, about three feet in front of the hood of my vehicle, making turns and leading me into my driveway. I just sat there and cried and thanked God. He had just showed me that He was guiding my path. He was and had been directing every step that I was taking. God had just answered another prayer and used His birds to demonstrate to me that He is always in control—of everything.

I also kept praying for God to open the doors that He wanted me to walk through and close and lock the doors that He wanted me to avoid. I did not realize at that time that He was giving me signs that that was exactly what He was doing.

One day while I was at work, I realized that everyday, as I approached a certain elevator, the doors would instantly open. I would walk up to it, and miraculously, it would open or already be open. Then, one day as I was walking toward that elevator near an unknown visitor, the man said to me, "That elevator seemed to be just sitting there waiting for us." I just laughed knowing that God did have it just waiting for me. Another day, I was orienting a nurse to a new position. As we were walking together, she started to go to an elevator closest to our location. I told her that I preferred walking a little farther because that other elevator always seemed more available to me. As we approached the elevator, the doors miraculously opened before we even got to it. She just looked at me and said, "Wow! You were right!" She had no idea that it was God opening the door for us.

I knew that God was telling me that He was opening the doors that He wanted me to walk through. He was guiding my path. He was in total control. I just kept thanking Him and praising Him for what He was doing for me.

I knew that God was still teaching me, guiding me, protecting me, and healing me. There is healing in His Presence, and I tried to spend as much time as possible in His Presence. I worked, went to church, went to the grocery store, spent time with my children, and spent time with the Lord. I was being accused of a lot of bad things which were not true, but I knew that God knew the truth. I did not need to defend myself. I just kept praying for total healing.

One night or early morning, I woke up suddenly from a dream that I had been crying uncontrollably with those heavy, deep, heart-felt, sobbing wails that I had experienced when we first separated several years before. The pain and sobbing that I felt in my dream was so real. I sat up immediately and felt my cheeks to see if I had actually been crying in my sleep and was surprised to find out that I was not crying, at least not in the natural.

Then I felt it! Deep within my soul, deep within my spirit, it was unbelievable and is still almost indescribable. I was sitting up, silent on my bed in the natural. But, those deep, retching, uncontrollable sobs that I was dreaming about were really happening very deep inside of me. I could feel what felt like my insides, my soul and my spirit, heaving, swaying back and forth like a rocking motion with those uncontrollable sobs and wails. I felt that my soul and spirit were in such intense pain and were crying out.

At first I thought that I was crazy. Then I thought to myself, "Oh, you have really lost it." But these sensations continued. I continued to feel my insides rock back and forth and cry in these uncontrollable, wailing sobs. I kept asking God to heal me totally from all the wounds of my past.

Then, I called my sister and tried to explain what was happening to me. She knew immediately. God had already revealed it to her.

She said that God had told her, "She was even more deeply wounded that you could ever imagine" and God said that the wounds of my past cut deep down beyond my emotions, to my soul and spirit, and I was in need of a very deep healing.

My sister could not understand why I had had such a hard time with the entire events of the past years. She could not understand why I had held on to a man that was obviously lying and manipulating me for decades. But, God had revealed the depth of my wounds to her so that she would have more patience with me and my healing. She also told me that God had once told her that the reason my ex-husband could manipulate me was that I had no self-esteem. I did not believe that I had any worth, so I felt that I was not worthy of more than I had settled for.

I have come to realize over the years that we are all sons and daughters of the Most High. God loves us all, but some of us don't love ourselves. We all deserve the best, but many of us settle for a lot less. I did not understand the traumatic effects of abuse and its wounds until recently. The best way to describe what I was feeling that early morning as my soul and spirit cried out is this:

The Body Level and abuse: Imagine a person that is repeatedly being physically stabbed. As the knife blade cuts through the skin, the fatty layers, the muscles, the bones, and the internal organs, more and more damage is being done to the victim's physical body.

The Soul Level and abuse: Imagine a person that is repeatedly being verbally and emotionally stabbed (abused). Those words cut just like a knife down to the soul or inner parts of the person—their thoughts, emotions, feelings, senses—all of their non-physical aspects that can not be touched by physical objects.

The Spirit Level and abuse: Imagine that person that has been stabbed (abused) and that knife has cut down to the deepest part of them, beyond the tissue or body and beyond even the non-physical parts or soul. These wounds get down to the very "heart" of the person—their spirit. It is our spirit that communes with the Spirit of God when in His presence. It is the part of us that truly makes us who we are. When our spirit is damaged, it affects who we are. (Some information from the website faithandhealth-connection.org)

These wounds to our soul and spirit are very real, but only God can see them and only God can heal them. This is a very real part of "the walking wounded," and it may be difficult to understand, unless someone has been hurt that deeply and has felt that almost indescribable pain or screaming, sobbing sensation from deep within your body. Unfortunately, anyone who has felt this also probably thought that she was crazy too. However, we are all multi-dimensional beings with a body, soul, and spirit. The process of healing of the wounds will not be complete in people until every dimension of them has been healed.

"For the word of God is alive and powerful. It is sharper than the sharpest two-edged sword, cutting between soul and spirit, between joint and marrow. It exposes our innermost thoughts and desires." Hebrews 4:12(NKJV)

CHAPTER 28

Soul Ties

"Keep away from angry, short-tempered people, or you will learn to be like them and endanger your soul."
Proverbs 22: 24-25 (NLT)

Our soul is a very real and important part of each of us. As previously discussed, our soul, deep within each of us, can become injured by people and events that occur in our lives. Our soul becomes invisibly attached to the souls of those we love or even fellowship with as family, friends, and pastors. A soul tie can be described as the joining together of minds and emotions in an unseen realm. These can be either good soul ties where God is kept as the center of the relationship or unhealthy soul ties which are a hindrance to a person.

Good soul ties or Godly soul ties are those that occur in a healthy relationship with similar believers in God. Good marriages, good friends, and good families are all examples of good soul ties which have good outcomes.

Bad or unhealthy soul ties are those that occur in bad relationships between parents, children, siblings, marriage partners, and even former sexual partners. These unhealthy soul ties can bring about a control over a person that can affect that person's life negatively. This happens even when young teenagers become sexually active. Once that door is open to having sex, it becomes hard to close leading to multiple sex partners at an early age as these teenagers date various people. It is like they are leaving a part of themselves behind with each sex partner.

Soul ties can also occur in different strengths depending on the length and depth of a relationship. These unseen ties can be compared to varying thicknesses of string or rope. New friends will have weak soul ties which are easily broken. Long time best friends will have stronger strength soul ties connecting their many years together. Newly married couples will have a depth to their relationship that ties them together because of their intimacy. However, the strongest and deepest soul ties are to those who have been married for a long time. These soul ties have a length (many years of friendship and marriage) and a depth (many years of marital relations and multiple children). These soul ties are a strong invisible force that links these people together in an unseen world. Consequently, when a long term marriage ends with abuse or infidelity, there is an invisible cord that keeps drawing these two people back together, almost like a bungee cord—when one tries to get away, this cords keeps pulling them back. Unfortunately for many of these hurt and wounded people, the healing can not be done until these invisible soul ties are broken off of them. (Some information from Untangling Damaging Soul Ties by Pastor Chris Simpson at www.newwineonline.com)

This is where my story continues again…

I could not understand why I kept getting pulled back into that relationship with my ex-husband. I could not understand why my heart ached so much like I had been stabbed repeatedly with a long knife in the chest.

I even said that it probably would not have hurt as much to be physically stabbed. I knew that the physical wounds would have healed much sooner than my deep emotional wounds were healing. He had harassed me, intimidated me, assaulted me, manipulated me, lied to me, cheated on me, raped me, stolen from me—every kind of abuse imaginable—but I kept wanting our relationship to be repaired. I wanted him to change so that our family could be together. Even months after the death threats had occurred, these feelings returned when I heard his voice. Our own children did not want him back in the house because of his abuse of all of us. But, I kept getting drawn back in, and I kept praying for God to deliver him from his abusive ways. I knew that I was living with a deep fear of him, and it did not make sense even to me that with one nice word or one nice gesture and I was suckered back under his control. I was so confused. I knew that at times I would go into panic mode just seeing his phone number or knowing that he was near. I would start crying and want to run away. Then other times, I was drawn into a desire to talk to him by just the look that he had or the tone in his voice. None of this made sense to me!

Sometimes, I thought that I was really crazy. I had been trapped in this emotional whirlwind and could not seem to get out of it. When I would try to get control back and gain my independence, his anger would increase and my fear of him would escalate. But it was like I was responding to his anger by being drawn back in more or maybe it was more like paralyzing fear that I could not seem to escape him. I had to get away, but I did not know how. I was an educated woman with a good income. I saw all the abuse on one hand but kept getting pulled back into a relationship with him. It was CRAZY!!!

It was not until I decided that I could not talk to him (and even feeling that God was telling me not to talk to him anymore) that my eyes were really being opened and the healing increased. I realized that the longer that I went without talking to him, the less I wanted to talk to him. Counselors and family had repeatedly told me this, but I felt trapped in that whirlwind or battle. I was getting stronger as I stayed away from him. I knew he was getting angrier and angrier since I no longer wanted to talk to him. My children and I all felt it. Several times, I had to warn him that I had a permanent restraining order so he could not harass me. I still feared him and kept my security alarm system for protection. Overall, the longer that I went without talking to him, the stronger that I was getting. I finally realized that the attachment from twenty-two plus years of marriage and three children were getting severed. His control over me was being broken.

I had always heard the word "soul tie" and had never put much thought into it. I related it to a feeling like soul music. However, I have come to learn through the years with all of the physical, emotional, and spiritual battles that I have been through, that these soul ties are real. There is a real spiritual bond or a bondage that ties you to another person. This soul tie or bondage is what pulls you back into the abuse as a victim and what causes a victim of abuse to possibly become an abuser. That is why children of abusive people, like my ex-husband, become abusers. That is why children of alcoholics, become alcoholics. That is why children of addicts, become addicts. That is why children that are molested possibly become child molesters. It is not only that all of these things and many others are learned behaviors; there is a real spiritual component to many things that can be passed down. The soul ties or generational ties, sometimes called generational curses, have to be broken off of a person to break the cycle that gets passed on to the next child, the next victim, the next wounded person.

Total healing can not occur until these soul ties or this bondage is broken. It is like a person being held hostage and being tied down with ropes or chains. They can not get free until the ropes or chains are removed. People are held spiritually bound to their abusers or anything in their past lives, until these real, invisible, spiritual ropes or bondage are removed from them. These soul ties will continue to pull them back like a bungee cord into that spiritual battle. That spiritual battle is also not visible to the naked eye, but it is very real. It is the battle of good versus evil. God is the only One who can free us from our chains of bondage. He is our Healer, and He is our Deliverer from all evil of our past.

CHAPTER 29

Moving Toward Wholeness

"Where there is no counsel, the people fall; but in the
multitude of counselors there is safety."
Proverbs 11:14 (NKJV)

Sometimes, the best thing that can happen for an abused person is a
fresh start or new beginning in a new area. The memories and ties to the
past can be so hurtful that sometimes making new memories is the best
healing—new friends, new schools, new jobs, etc. Hopefully, the victim
has a supportive family that she can go to live with or near to begin a new
life. It is much easier when there is one person to consider, but when you
are relocating an entire family, it becomes much more difficult. It is much
better for the family if they can all agree to relocate. One thing a parent
does not want to do is to cause more hurting or wounds to a child who has
already been hurt. That is why counseling and having an advocate for the
child is very important.

It is a very difficult decision when considering uprooting a family
who has been in one location for many years. Leaving family, friends,

house, job, and everything familiar can be overwhelming. However, it can ultimately also be a relief to escape the fear that some victims live with in an area.

Fear is not a tangible thing that can be touched; however, it is very real. It touches a person's life and affects their responses to many things. Fear is a real response to a perceived threat or danger; it is usually resulting from an actual threat or danger. Fear is learned from experience and causes both psychological and physical responses to a person. There can be triggers that initiate the fear response in a person.

The best thing to prevent these episodes of fear is to avoid or eliminate those triggers and continue counseling. When something or someone is causing the fear response, move away from it. More healing can occur when a victim separates from those triggers and continues getting counseling, especially spiritual counseling.

This is where my story continues again…

My children and I were feeling more and more anger. Their dad was always fussing and yelling. They still avoided his calls many times, making excuses to not answer the phone. They tried to minimize their contact with him. Then some days, he would just show up to pick them up. This always triggered a panic mode in me. I had always encouraged them to talk to him which got me in trouble many times when he would verbally attack them. I was living with fear and could not escape it. I kept feeling that someone was watching and waiting—just like the doughnuts and newspaper under my carport. The children and I kept telling the counselors what we were experiencing, and they kept telling us to move away. Family and friends were telling us to move away, but we had just built a beautiful new house, and the children loved their friends and neighborhood.

The turmoil around us continued. I kept reaching out to God to help us. I prayed that God would bring peace to our house or move us—all of us—I did not want to leave anyone behind. I knew that God had moved us to a new part of town the year before, but I knew that we were not far enough.

My oldest son was a senior in high school that year. He did not have much to do with his dad. He had not been invited to his dad's wedding, and his dad made minimal effort to talk to him. He had watched and seen the immoral behavior of his dad over the last few years and had lost respect for him. I kept reminding him that his dad did love him and that he needed to try to have a relationship with him.

On senior night with his football team, my son did not want his dad with him on the field—he had not even told him about it. As my son and I were standing on the field, we could see his dad, all dressed for the event, and his family sitting in the stands and very angry. There was not a smile on their faces. Their anger was intensifying. I was later accused of keeping their dad off the field and away from the children. That family never bothered to ask my son about that night. They never asked any of our children why they did not go to his wedding a few months before. That family would have heard the truth from the children if any of them had even ever asked for it. They just blamed me for everything.

My youngest son started feeling the urge to move away from the entire area. He was feeling this turmoil with his dad and even in his school. His dad had made another suicidal comment to him, and he had not been able to sleep for days. He told the counselor and me that he was sensing increasing danger. At his young age, he also feared his dad's potential for violence. He wanted me to purchase a gun for protection. He even told the counselor and me that he would rather kill his dad if needed, than for his dad to kill me. My son was beginning to feel the danger that I had been feeling without me saying anything to him about it. He asked me why his dad could not be like his friend's dad who was a Godly role-model to my son. My son had turned to God and God was increasing his sensitivity to the spiritual world.

My youngest child, my daughter, at first did not want to move. Then, the girls in her school all started turning against her. Her best friend from as far back as day care when they were toddlers had even gotten upset with her. She started crying that she wanted to move, now—she did not even want to wait till school finished that year.

I kept telling the children that we could not leave anyone behind. We kept praying that my oldest would want to move after graduation. He actually had been considering moving with us and, then changed his mind after talking to his friends. I kept telling God that I could not leave him.

Then when school was almost over, on Mother's Day, I went to our Spirit-filled church. I know that God spoke to me again about our situation. I heard:

"Mothers—God has a plan for your sons. Don't you know that Moses' mother was heart-broken when she had to leave him in that basket in the water? But the Lord told her to leave him and go home—He had a plan for the child… Don't you know that Hannah's heart was broken when she had to leave Samuel at the temple? But God told her to turn around and go home. Leave the child—I have a plan for him. These mothers did not want to leave their sons, but God knew what was best. He told the mothers to leave and go home. He told them that He had a plan for their sons' life and He would provide for them."

Then, to confirm that he was talking about my oldest son, he started talking about the exact month and year that my son was born, eighteen years before.

I was shaking and crying. I knew that God was giving me a message to leave and go back "home" to my family that I had left many years before. I knew that He was telling me to leave my son and that He would provide for him. God told me that he had a plan for my son.

My children and I sat down and discussed what I knew that God was telling me. We all cried because we did not want to leave my oldest behind, but we knew that we needed to walk in obedience. Many family and friends had been telling me to relocate for years to get away from my ex and his family. Moving across town was not far enough. Now, my youngest son was feeling the danger lurking that I had felt for many years and felt a need to protect us.

I started looking for a job and almost immediately got a call. Everything would transfer from my current job. I was told by my attorney that I had to notify my ex by phone and in writing, which the attorney took care of, as well as a petition to the court to allow the children to move out of the area. Even my attorney had told me for years that I needed to get away from that area to a safe place. However, that step to make that verbal contact with my ex-husband was terrifying. I called him, while recording it, to inform him that two of our children and I would be moving. He was very angry since he did not see much of them already. I informed him that the decision was just recently made, and I would be starting the process.

His anger was intensifying daily. The children could sense his anger every time that they talked to him. My children were not feeling safe and verbalized this to their counselor. The counselor told me that according to what the children were telling her, she felt that their dad was unpredictable and dangerous at that time. He was losing more control and his anger was intensifying. She told me to not allow the children to go with their dad due to the potential for violence at that time. She even contacted my attorney with her concerns.

I had a job offer for a transfer and then got a call from a prophetic person at our church before I even accepted the offer. She told me that God had just told her to give me a message; He said,

"The door is now open—you just need to walk through it!"

I realized that God had been opening elevator doors for me at work. Now He was opening a door for a new job in a different location, near my family. God had told me to move and leave my son behind, something that I never wanted to do. God had told me that their dad would never change. The fear that I had felt for years was now getting felt by my children. I knew that God was still protecting us. My children and I knew that we had to walk in obedience for God's blessings.

CHAPTER 30

Obedience

"For I know the plans that I have for you," says the Lord.
"They are plans for good, not for disaster, to give you a future
and a hope." Jeremiah 29:11 (NLT)

God blesses obedience to Him. To walk in obedience is to walk in faith, knowing that wherever God leads you, He will take care of you. Abraham was blessed by his obedience to God, even to the point of almost killing his own son, and became the father of many nations. Mary walked in obedience and was blessed with giving birth to the Son of God. Noah walked in obedience to build a huge ark for a flood, despite everyone thinking that he was crazy, and saved his family and animals of all types from destruction. These are just a few of the examples of walking in obedience. Only God knows the future, and He always plans for good for everyone. When someone knows that God has spoken to him/her and has given them a directive, the important thing is to walk in the direction that the Lord has spoken and He will guide the steps. The divine blessings may not be evident immediately, but God will bless those who walk in obedience and faith, knowing that He is always in control and has good plans for all of them.

This is where my story continues again…

I had clearly heard from the Lord to move "home" and leave my son. Again, God answers prayers, but sometimes it is not the way that we hope and pray for. My youngest son told me one day while bringing him to school that "some of God's greatest gifts are unanswered prayers." Immediately after he said this, that song started playing on the radio. We both looked at each other and knew that God had given us confirmation of what my son had just said. We just have to trust that God knows best and will do what He says, no matter how hard it is. That is part of walking in obedience.

My two youngest children and I left our big, beautiful new home and a big part of our heart behind when we left my oldest son, their big brother. My children had repeatedly said that he had been more of a father-figure to them than their own dad. He was patient and kind with them, unlike their dad. My son stayed in our new home there while the realtor tried to sell it. We moved to the place where God lead us and eventually bought the old house that God told me to buy. We just kept praying for God to move quickly, change my son, and bring my son back to us to be a family again. I kept thanking God for what He was doing in our lives. I kept feeling that God's hand of protection was over us.

Many things happened while we were apart that opened our eyes even more to the miraculous. My youngest children attended a Christian school while their brother attended college back where we had moved from. We went to the church where God lead us with the school, and we were surrounded by Godly Christian people. We went into Christian counseling with a Deliverance Ministry. Many, many people were praying for us in our new location as well as our old. Generational ties and curses were being broken off of us. My Godly friends that I had left behind in our church there were reaching out to my son. He was having fun with his friends, but he was missing us, his family, more. My son was right in the middle of a spiritual warfare with good versus evil battling for his soul.

My son started seeing the difference when he was with us. There was a peace in our house, the presence of God. This was so different than the turmoil that had surrounded us in that area before. Even my realtor was getting harassing calls again about my new house. She was experiencing the "warfare" that had been attacking us. Their dad was still fussing and cussing, but we were several hours away from him now. We now had a buffer zone where he would probably not just show up unexpectedly. This was a tremendous relief to my children and me. The fear was finally subsiding. We prayed together as a family and sought the Lord together. God started revealing Himself to my son. Whereas before, my son thought that we were all was crazy, God was now showing my son exactly the things that I had been trying to teach him. God was revealing the spiritual world and revealing the miraculous to my son. My son was learning the real power of prayer when you have an intimate relationship with our Lord.

God did exactly what He said that He would do. He had a plan for my son and all of us. He had provided for my son while we were apart with Godly role- models to teach him. He had turned my son's heart to Him. God brought the buyer for my house after almost a year, about the same time that my son finished his first year of college and wanted to move to be with us. My son moved one weekend and got several prophetic words from several of God's prophets that he met that same weekend. My children and I were now all in the same place spiritually. We all knew that God had a calling on our lives. We were not sure of His plan, but we continued to walk together in obedience, as a family and as a team.

CHAPTER 31

Wholeness

"Today I have given you the choice between life and death, between bless-ings and curses. I call on heaven and earth to witness the choice you make. Oh, that you would choose life, that you and your descendants might live!"
Deuteronomy 30:19 (NLT)

Walking in obedience is the key to walking out God's plan in our lives. God had never promised that it would be an easy path. Jesus came to this earth knowing the plan for crucifixion of his life, knowing the pain and suffering that He would endure, but also knowing that it was the ultimate plan for the salvation of mankind. Many times, as humans, we take a wrong path or usually the path of least resistance or easiest which is usu-ally to "go with the flow" onto a worldly path. This is where we are in error. God's path may not be easy, but it is rich in blessings for those who seek Him and His guidance for every step that they take. We do make mistakes, but God does promise to use everything that is meant for harm and turn it around for the good for those who love Him and seek His will. The Bible also says that we go through tribulations so that we can provide comfort to those who will go through similar tribulations. I now know why I am at this point in my life today.

As I wrote in the first chapters of this book, I had been told many times over the years that I should write a book. I had even written a book many years ago, never publishing it and eventually destroying it. In the last few days, as I was writing the last chapters, I felt God leading me to read my many journals where I had made note after note of our thoughts and feelings as well as all of these events as they were occurring in our lives over the years. It reminded me of the total confusion, the total craziness, and the total turmoil that we lived under as that battle of good versus evil was being fought for me and my children. We did not understand spiritual warfare, but we were living in the middle of it. We did not understand soul ties and generational curses, but we were struggling and fighting in that unseen battle. I knew that God had rescued us and protected us as I felt His hand of protection over us. I knew that God had surrounded us with His Godly people to minister to us and guide us. I knew that God was healing and delivering my children and me as He broke the chains of bondage to alcoholism and abuse from us. I also found out after we moved that God had to break the generational curse of murder/ suicide when my youngest son finally told me and a spiritual counselor that he had planned for a long time to kill his own father and then kill himself. He had actually sat on a bed with a loaded gun waiting on several occasions to murder his abusive dad. My ex-husband had always said that the children were fine and refused to help pay for what he considered "needless counseling." I thank God that I continued to try to get help for my children and me. I could not see how much my own children were hurting in that emotional turmoil that we were in, which we now know was a spiritual warfare. I did not know at the time that just like physical traits are passed down, generational curses are passed down through each new generation until they are broken. I also know that we are still a "work in progress" with a plan for total healing and total deliverance. The wounds that I have suffered, as well as some of my children, were deep and are still being healed layer by layer. We have prayed for total purification that we would be pure vessels for God to use in His kingdom.

EDITOR'S NOTES
The writing of this book:

"Now faith is the substance of things hoped for,
the evidence of things not seen."
Hebrews 11:1 (NKJV)

I have already said that I did not want to write this book. I did not want to hurt anyone with my story, and I did not want to open that door to my past that had been closed. However, something recently happened that triggered a fear to return in my life. Yes, my children and I still do battle in spiritual warfare, but we have grown in knowledge about it and the Armor of God (Ephesians 6:11-18). Their dad has not changed yet, still making comments occasionally about wanting to kill himself and getting drunk, even telling our children in his drunkenness this past year that he still loves me and misses me. He still drinks excessively, especially when he is not with his wife. We still all pray for him and his family. We know that they were all abused as well and do not realize that they function out of wounds from their past. We continue to pray for all members of my family as well, that all wounds of abuse will be healed and the cycle of abuse will be broken from everyone. We have all been victims of abuse over the years;

however, it was not about that abuse that affected me this time. A trigger in my life recently caused these feelings of fear and anxiety to return. I knew that God had healed me from these feelings. I realize that it is a new abuse, an abuse not written about much. One that is still being concealed by many …

The abuse that I felt God was revealing to me is the abuse that is increasingly occurring in the workplace with bosses or superiors intimidating, harassing, fussing, yelling, threatening, or needlessly criticizing (in other words, abusing) their innocent, hard-working employees while secretly planning or scheming actions against them to remove them from their jobs. This has recently happened to me, and this different type of abuse has now affected me—workplace or economic abuse!

I had been told a month before by a corporate director that my boss was "abusing" me and "blaming" me for things that were not my fault. I was told then that I was doing a good job. She also said that she could tell that I had been an abused woman by the way that I was always trying to please my boss, working incessantly and avoiding confrontation. She said that I was doing "nothing wrong" and that I needed to "stand up for myself." Despite my feelings that he was trying to fire me, she assured me that I would not be fired. However, I lost my job a month later. I knew that God had already sent someone to tell me the truth. I knew that I kept getting woken up at times with different scriptures referring to scheming or things being done in darkness. God knows everything that is done, even in darkness. There are no secrets from God. I also know that the day that I lost my job, I got a call from one of God's prophets who told me that the Lord sent me a message saying that "He has rescued me from Egypt and rescued me from Pharaoh who was abusing me." I feel that more and more people are going to become victim to this type of economic abuse as the end times come. The Word says that "What can be shaken, will be shaken." However, I also know that those who truly seek the Lord, no matter what happens around them, He will protect and provide for them—they have to just walk in faith. I have realized that this has been a test of faith, and though I fell apart and was very "shaken", I now wait patiently for the Lord to open the door to the job that He wants me to have, remembering that "Faith is the substance of things hoped for, the evidence of things not seen."

I felt compelled to review my old journals this week as I neared completion of this book and found several entries written many years ago that made me realize that God was reminding me of some things that I had forgotten. Years ago, I kept writing that I felt that God was telling me to write a book about abuse to help other abused women. I had written it in obedience but then destroyed it, probably in disobedience. I actually wrote that these abused women were walking around wounded. Oh my God! That is why this title came to my mind—**The Walking Wounded.** I also found an entry where I was given a Word from God when my children and I moved near my family to escape the abuse. The message was that **"God had rescued us from Egypt."** I knew that God had rescued me from Egypt or abuse not once, but twice. Then, I found a prophecy given to me from a prophet in an international ministry saying, "The Lord said that one day I would be "helping abused women with God's Word." Lastly, I found an entry where I had written the name of a future ministry to help abused woman and children. I know that God has a plan for my children and me. However, I know that everything is in God's timing, not ours. We just need to keep walking in obedience and faith as we wait on the Lord.

There were so many traumas that I had vividly remembered. However, I had forgotten these words from God—these plans for my future. I know that God is always in control. I wrote this book in obedience to God again, while I keep applying for jobs weekly, interviewing, and praying for Him to open the door for the job that He wants me to get. He has opened doors before, and I walk in faith that He will open the door again. My children and I have already been blessed by God's protection and provision through all of the abuse. We have seen the mighty hand of God in our everyday life in many things not mentioned in this book. We have gotten many prophecies over the years with the miraculous plans from God. However, as a family and as a team, my children and I continue to pray for God to direct each step that we take as we try to walk the path that He has planned for us. We know that everything that we go through is training and preparing us for His ultimate purpose for our lives.

PRAYER

A Prayer for all the Abused

"But you, when you pray, go into your room, and when you have shut your door, pray to your Father who is in the Secret Place, and your Father who sees in secret will reward you openly."
Matthew 6:6 (NKJV)

"He that dwell in the Secret Place of the Most High, shall abide in the Shadow of the Almighty."
Psalm 91:1 (NKJV)

I know that I was given a directive or mandate from God to write this book to reach out to the abused people of this world. There are also many people abused because of race or religion. As I reviewed my journals, I found entries for many years where my children and I prayed together for all the abused, just like my family had prayed for us. We thank God for rescuing us from a life of abuse and delivering us from the spiritual bondage that we were under. I know that there are so many people that do not know this yet and would not even understand this. Many will even think that I am crazy. However, I can only tell each one of you that there is so much more than we can see with the natural eyes and only God can reveal the supernatural to you. I know that many women and children secretly cry out at night in the darkness, just as I did, for God to rescue them. I have felt that feeling of total hopelessness and being trapped, not knowing how to get away. As I have grown in my relationship with God, I now know that the secret is to develop an intimacy with God, not just an occasional visitation when we need Him, knowing that Christ is our Lord and Savior who died on the cross and rose from the dead for the forgiveness of our sins and His Holy Spirit still lives in those of us who believe and reach out to Him today. As we reach out to God, He will reach out to us. Seek Him day and night. Ask for Him to reveal more of Himself. Ask for His miraculous intervention in your life. God is no respecter of persons and what He had done for me and my children, He will do for all of those who seek Him and His will for their lives.

My prayer is that every abused person—man, woman, or child—that reads this book will get a miraculous touch from God. I pray that every heart will turn to our Lord, Jesus Christ. I pray for total healing from all the invisible wounds of abuse. I pray for total deliverance from evil and all the generational curses from the past (The Lord's Prayer). I pray that what God has done for me and my children that He will do for each of you. Lastly, I pray that every person reading this book will develop a true intimacy with God, learning the importance of getting into His Presence in the secret place of the Most High (Psalm 91)…

It is in this Secret Place that we can all be *__His Secret Angels.__*

The two prayers that I repeatedly prayed are Psalm 91 and The Lord's Prayer from the New King James Version.

Psalm 91 (recited as a prayer to God)
    I dwell in the Place called Secret

Abiding under my Almighty's Shadow
He is my Refuge and Fortress—I trust Him
Surely He delivers me from the snare of the fowler
And from perilous pestilence
He covers me with His Feathers
As I take refuge under His Wing
His Truth is my Shield and Buckler
I am not afraid of terror by night
Nor arrow by day
Nor pestilence walking in darkness
Nor destruction that lays waste at noontime
A thousand fall at my side and ten-thousand at
      my right hand
But none ever come near me
Only my eyes see the wicked's reward
Because The Lord is my Refuge—
The Most High my Habitation
NO evil befalls me
Nor does any plague come near me or my dwelling
His Angels have charge over me
And keep me in ALL His Ways
They hold me up in their hands so I
      cannot dash a stone
I tread on lions and cobras
And trample young lions and serpents
Because my total love is set on Him
He delivers me
He sets me on high because I intimately know Him
I call on Him and He answers

He is with me in trouble and delivers and honors me
I am satisfied with long life and shown His Wonderful Salvation

The Lord's Prayer
Our Father,
Who art in Heaven,
Hallowed be thy Name.
Thy Kingdom come,
Thy will be done,
on earth,
As it is in Heaven.
Give us this day,
our daily bread.
And forgive us our trespasses,
As we forgive those who trespass against us.
And lead us not into temptation,
But deliver us from evil.
For thine is the Kingdom,
The Power, and the Glory,
Forever and ever.
Amen.